GET UNSTUCK

Sunder Ramachandran is chief people and transformation officer and head of corporate communications at Biological E. Ltd. He has led teams across India and emerging markets in senior roles at GSK and Dr. Reddy's Laboratories. He is the co-author of *HeadStart* (2024) and writes on business and leadership for publications including *The Economic Times*, *Financial Express* and *The Hindu Business Line*. Sunder is an Eisenhower Fellow and a Chartered Fellow of the CIPD (FCIPD). He holds an MBA from Macquarie Graduate School of Management, Australia, and an MSc in Human Resources from the University of Leicester, UK.

Advance Praise from Managers Who Made the Leap

Mid-career leaders share how working with Sunder turned steady performance into visible impact, broadened their range and strengthened their confidence to operate as leaders.

'Sunder asked me one question that reframed my career: "Are you building systems others operate, or are you the recognised architect?" I realised I was the invisible engine behind major decisions, but never the name associated with them. His frameworks helped me own the narrative without becoming loud. Six months later I was leading cross-functional strategy. A year later I became CFO. This book gives you the question and the path to the answer.'
—*Manoj Jayawardena, CFO, Rockland Distilleries, Colombo*

'For years I believed my work would speak for itself. It did, but only to the people closest to it. Sunder's coaching showed me the difference between self-promotion and meaningful visibility. The goal was never to look good; it was to make impact legible to decision-makers. If you are a strong middle manager who keeps getting overlooked, this is the playbook you have been missing.'
—*Nirupa Janaka Kumara, Former HR Director, Coca-Cola, Colombo*

'During Sri Lanka's economic collapse, I assumed my job was risk control. As our country GM, Sunder pushed a sharper lens: strategic insurance. His volatility tools helped me turn compliance into competitive advantage, with early-warning routines that surfaced issues weeks before they hit. If you are technically strong but stuck, this book will change how you think about leadership.'
—*Ravindi Ratnayake, Senior Manager, Group Compliance and Healthcare BU Compliance Lead, DKSH, Bangkok*

'Coaching with Sunder taught me to act before I felt perfectly ready. I took stretch assignments, moved into new roles and learnt to

influence how work gets done across the enterprise. The real shift was from dependable executor to trusted partner. My confidence grew, my priorities sharpened and new opportunities opened to drive enterprise-wide outcomes.'
—*Alok Dubey, Lead L&D Operations, GSK*

'When the Sri Lankan economy collapsed in 2021, most leaders focused only on survival. Sunder taught us to focus on what we could control and to lead with steadiness. He helped us hold performance when salaries had lost 60% of their value. That capability gets noticed. People who can keep teams together under pressure do not stay middle managers for long.'
—*Tyrone Fernando, Head of Operations, A. Baur & Co., Colombo*

'I was the marketing expert who could not escape the marketing box. Strategic conversations excluded me because I was "the brand guy". Sunder's coaching taught me to demonstrate range without abandoning my core strength. I volunteered for projects outside my domain and brought marketing thinking to operations. That opened doors I had been locked out of for years. This book shows you how to break out of your box.'
—*Prasad Magammana, Commercial Operations Manager, GSK, London*

'The biggest shift for me was moving from "I need to know and do everything" to leading through clarity, influence and trust. Sunder pushed me to engage senior leaders with confidence and to invest in transferable skills and not just functional depth. That mindset change expanded my scope, increased my trust in the team and gave me a steadier presence in the room. It also made role transitions feel natural rather than risky.'
—*Dr Kanika Singh, Senior Manager L&D, GSK*

GET UNSTUCK

BREAKING THROUGH THE MIDDLE-MANAGEMENT PLATEAU

SUNDER RAMACHANDRAN

WESTLAND
BUSINESS

WESTLAND
BUSINESS

Published by Westland Business, an imprint of Westland Books, a division of Nasadiya Technologies Private Limited, in 2026

No. 269/2B, First Floor, 'Irai Arul', Vimalraj Street, Nethaji Nagar, Alapakkam Main Road, Maduravoyal, Chennai 600095

Westland, the Westland logo, Westland Business and the Westland Business logo are the trademarks of Nasadiya Technologies Private Limited, or its affiliates.

Copyright © Sunder Ramachandran, 2026

Sunder Ramachandran asserts the moral right to be identified as the author of this work.

ISBN: 9789371979733

10 9 8 7 6 5 4 3 2 1

The views and opinions expressed in this work are the author's own and the facts are as reported by him, and the publisher is in no way liable for the same.

All rights reserved

Typeset by Mukul

Printed at Parksons Graphics Pvt. Ltd

No part of this book may be reproduced, or stored in a retrieval system, or transmitted in any form or by any means, electronic, mechanical, photocopying, recording, or otherwise, without express written permission of the publisher.

*To Deeksha and Veda: my constant sponsors in the
only roles that truly matter*

Contents

Introduction: Get Unstuck   xi
My Lens and Limitations   xix
Looking One Step Ahead   xxi

PART 1
FOUNDATION: Building Your Core Capabilities

Section 1: Volatility Navigation: Turning Noise into Signals and Speed

1. The Storm Is the Strategy   5
2. The Volatility Navigator   17
3. View from the Top with Rajiv Jayaraman, Founder-CEO, KNOLSKAPE   27
4. Do-It Notes: Your Volatility Navigation Road Map   30

Section 2: Anchored in Values: Making Values a Competitive Advantage

5. When Values Get Tested   37
6. The Values Edge   47
7. View from the Top with Annaswamy Vaidheesh, Former MD, GSK Pharmaceuticals and J&J India   58
8. Do-It Notes: Your Values Leadership Road Map   61

PART 2
NAVIGATION: Advancing Through Complexity

Section 3: Leveraging Global–Local Dynamics: Translating Global Strategy into Local Wins

9. The Global–Local Tug of War   69

10. The Both-And Solution 79
11. View from the Top with Hariram Krishnan, Former MD, Galderma India 89
12. Do-It Notes: Your Global–Local Navigation Road Map 93

Section 4: Unique Reputation: Making Yourself Visible and in Demand

13. When Reputation Becomes Reality 101
14. The Reputation Architect 112
15. View from the Top with Vinita Vasanth, MD, Lifesciences, Accenture 123
16. Do-It Notes: Your Reputation-Building Road Map 126

PART 3
IMPACT: Leading at Scale

Section 5: Exceptional Teams: Building Leaders Who Build Leaders

17. When Teams Transcend Individuals 135
18. Teams That Grow Leaders 142
19. View from the Top with Vikas Dua, Head of People, Weber Shandwick 157
20. Do-It Notes: Your Team-Building Road Map 160

Section 6: Sustainable Transformation: Delivering Change That Sticks and Scales

21. Building the Transformation Muscle 167
22. The Transformation Architect 176
23. View from the Top with Vivek Gambhir, Venture Partner, Lightspeed India, Former CEO, Godrej Consumer Products & boAt Lifestyle 189
24. Do-It Notes: Your Transformation Road Map 192

Conclusion 197
Acknowledgements 201

Introduction: Get Unstuck

You've likely paused in the middle of a work day or while making a report, reflected on your current career stage and wondered if this is as far as you will go. You've delivered results, built expertise and earned trust, yet your career feels stuck. A quiet restlessness lingers. It surfaces after a big win, simmers during a routine catch-up with your boss or grips you on the long commute home. You are not failing, but you are not moving forward either.

Meanwhile, younger colleagues land stretch assignments, and your peers step into more strategic roles. You continue to earn solid ratings year after year and receive interesting projects, but there is no real movement up the ladder.

Every senior leader you admire once sat exactly where you sit now. They felt the same restlessness. Faced the same political complexity. Wondered if they had what it took. The difference wasn't talent or luck alone; it was deciding to stop waiting for permission and start building their path to leadership.

That restlessness is telling you something. It's ambition in disguise. Listen to it.

Who This Book Is For

You're a mid-career professional with twelve to twenty years under your belt. Maybe you're a senior manager eyeing an AVP role, a functional director ready for Profit & Loss (P&L) responsibility, a leader seeking bigger impact, or someone who knows they're capable of more but can't break through. You know your decisions could shape more than just your team, yet nothing seems to move the needle. So, what's keeping you stuck?

Well, three shifts changed the game while you were busy delivering results:

Delayering killed the ladder. Organisations flattened dramatically. There are fewer senior roles than capable people. Artificial intelligence (AI) and faster talent cycles mean coasting is career suicide. That comfortable climb you expected no longer exists.

Digital transformation shrank the room for specialists. You can't just be good at one thing anymore. Leaders are expected to balance margins and morale, vision and execution, revenue and reputation. The single-function expert is sidelined.

Excellence stopped standing out. Doing great work isn't enough. You need to translate between C-suite vision and frontline reality. You need to be the integrator, the translator, the one who creates clarity from chaos. Functional excellence without visibility keeps you stuck.

I Have Been There

I have made this leap. From running a function at a country level to running it regionally. Then a full P&L as country general manager (GM). And after years as a VP and SVP in global organisations, I eventually stepped into a CXO role.

In 2019, I was stuck in a functional leadership role at a global pharmaceutical company. I had been an entrepreneur for five

Introduction   xiii

years earlier in my career. Those skills should have been enough for P&L leadership, I thought. But every internal application got overlooked. The gap between running your own small business and leading inside a complex organisation was massive.

It took two years to crack the code. An executive coach helped me see my blind spots. A few painful mistakes taught me what not to do. And yes, luck played a part when the Sri Lanka country GM role opened in December 2020. Finally, I'd broken through the middle-management plateau. I owned the full P&L with every function reporting in, and the buck stopped with me. It was exhilarating.

The high did not last. In my first country leadership meeting, I sat across from the finance director, debating investment trade-offs. My process optimisation skills were not enough to decide whether to reduce a marketing budget or delay a product launch. I could model the ROI of each option, but I couldn't read which decision would cost me political capital with the regional head or tank team morale. I was skilled at making my function better, not how to steer the business.

I reached out to a peer leader who had navigated a similar transition a year before me. He helped me see what the business needed, not just what I was good at. Those conversations stuck with me. They became the 'looking one step ahead' approach in this book.

Sri Lanka then entered its worst economic and political crisis in history. That GM role became a leadership crucible. What should have taken a decade to learn got compressed into two years. The crisis stripped away theory and left only what works. Many stories in this book emerge from that period for exactly this reason.

What Makes This Book Different

This isn't a pep talk about thinking big. You already do that. What you need is what actually works inside real companies. Think like an owner, act like a connector and learn to navigate the politics of growth.

This is a field guide written by someone who made the leap recently enough to remember every stumble. To use a cricket analogy, think of this book as insights from a player on the field rather than commentary from the broadcast booth.

After coaching dozens of managers, I noticed a pattern: six capabilities where the successful ones focused their energy. Not everyone mastered all six, and some took different paths to leadership, but these showed up often enough to be a solid starting point. I call it the **VALUES** framework:

1. Volatility Navigation
2. Anchored in Values
3. Leveraging Global–Local Dynamics
4. Unique Reputation
5. Exceptional Teams
6. Sustainable Transformation

Each section, based on one of these values, follows a consistent four-chapter structure designed to move you from insight to action:

- *Chapter 1: Real-world stories* showing the messy decisions, political navigation and hard-won lessons that shape the reality of middle management.
- *Chapter 2: Practical, repeatable frameworks* field-tested for managers without full authority and built to signal readiness for leadership roles.
- *Chapter 3: View from the top*, featuring senior leaders on how they spot managers ready for bigger roles.
- *Chapter 4: Do-it notes* for what to do this month, this quarter, this year. Specific moves that make you visible as someone ready for leadership.

Introduction   xv

You can read straight through or jump to the section addressing your current challenge. Each section stands alone, and together the **VALUES** framework forms a complete system for advancement.

The Backstory Behind the Do-It Notes

These notes appear at the end of every section for a reason, and their origin traces back to a single conversation that changed how I coach and lead. In 2021, a few months into my Sri Lanka GM role, three members of my leadership team were selected for a global development programme that combined masterclasses, group coaching and a monthly thirty-minute check-in with their manager. I met each of them every month to review what they had learned, to observe how their leadership showed up in the previous four weeks and to agree on what they would try next so the learning would not remain abstract.

Our HR director, Nirupa, often joined these sessions and stayed behind after one of them. I had just told our finance director, Manoj Jayawardena, that he should connect ideas more clearly and contribute more actively in meetings. Nirupa said my intent was right but the feedback was not landing, and when I asked why, she explained that it was too abstract and that I needed to be specific about what to do in the next thirty days, what to build over the next quarter and what to lock in over the year. I tried that framing the very next week, and the effect was immediate because the managers now knew where to begin, how to build momentum and how to show progress in reviews. That conversation is the source of the Do-It Notes, and I owe that shift to Nirupa, a former colleague who became a friend. The structure now lives in this book so you can use it the same way: start now, build rhythm and make your growth visible.[1]

---

1   See 'Nirupa Janaka Kumara', LinkedIn, http://linkedin.com/in/nirupa-janaka-kumara-9a676132/; 'Manoj Jayawardena', LinkedIn, http://lk.linkedin.com/in/manoj-jayawardena-rockland.

The Middle Managers You Will Meet

Throughout this book, you will follow the stories of three middle managers, composites drawn from dozens of professionals I have coached over the years. Their challenges and breakthroughs are real. I chose them because they started from different points, faced distinct obstacles and figured out how to break through.

Priya, thirty-six, built her career in commercial banking across South Asia. Her data models drove millions in revenue. Her analytics shaped regional strategy. Yet she remained invisible, making others successful while staying in the background. Classic analytical trap: essential but unseen.

Arjun, thirty-eight, spent fourteen years in pharmaceutical R&D across India and Southeast Asia. He became everyone's crisis manager. The person you approached when projects failed. The one who always came to the rescue. That reliability had become his cage: indispensable but not promotable.

Kavita, forty, had mastered consumer goods brand marketing across Southeast Asian markets, translating global campaigns for local success. Yet she kept being seen as creative rather than commercial. Her strength had become her weakness: it limited her advancement to strategic roles.

They found practical ways to break through. You will witness the exact moments when they stopped thinking like specialists and started thinking like business leaders, and what they did to make it permanent.

Before You Begin

Here are three reflection questions to consider. Don't rush to answer them now. Let them simmer as you read. By the end, you will have clarity and a plan.

- Which leaders in your organisation do you admire and why?
- What would you need to change about yourself to compete for the next level?
- If you were promoted tomorrow, what would you stop doing?

Let's get you unstuck and into the leadership role you're ready for.

My Lens and Limitations

Every writer brings perspectives and biases that shape how we see the world. Here are mine.

What I Assume

- *You want to advance, but on your own terms.* I assume most readers want greater impact and influence. Some will choose deeper expertise over authority. Others will trade scale for balance. This book focuses on moving up. If that's not your path right now, the frameworks still help you understand what senior leaders look for.
- *Being stuck is a problem.* I write about 'stuckness' as a problem, but some plateaus are chosen and valuable. Taking a pause to consolidate, reflect or recover isn't wrong. The risk lies in remaining there by default.
- *The system is imperfect but navigable.* Organisations are political, with fewer senior roles than capable people. Capability building improves your odds. Nothing guarantees outcomes, but preparation improves probabilities.

Where I am Biased

- *Survivorship bias.* I'm writing from the winner's circle. I studied those who made the leap, including myself. I didn't study the equally capable who didn't make it. That shapes the patterns I've drawn.
- *Privilege of access.* My path had advantages I can't unwind. Quality education, roles at global MNCs, structured development programmes and strong mentors and sponsors. I've extracted principles that should transcend privilege, but I can't fully separate them.
- *Action bias.* I lean towards action. My instinct is to test and adjust rather than making perfect plans first, and that is demonstrated in many of the stories and tools in the book.
- *Gender bias.* I can acknowledge but cannot fully understand the barriers that women face. I have learnt from female colleagues and incorporated their perspectives, but my frameworks reflect my easier path I've experienced through certain doors.

Why This Matters

Now you know where I'm coming from. Take what works, challenge what doesn't. Test these ideas in your reality. Treat this book as a sparring partner, not a script.

Now, let's dive into the lessons that shaped it.

Looking One Step Ahead

Early in my career, I made a classic middle-management mistake: I went directly to top executives—CXOs inside or outside my organisation—for advice. They were generous with their time, giving me thirty minutes of undivided attention that left me inspired, even awed. The next morning at my desk, I was still stuck. Their advice was strategic, but it felt like getting directions to climb Everest when I was still figuring out the stairs.

This changed when I became country GM for Sri Lanka at a leading pharmaceutical MNC and I called Wael Chourbaji,[1] then GM for Lebanon and Jordan, who had been in the role for a year. Wael had two decades of commercial management experience, and more importantly, he was just one step ahead. He knew which relationships mattered in the first month, how to handle the first budget review and which regional leaders to win over early. He showed me how to run monthly business reviews for impact. Every call ended with two things I could put to use right away.

That's 'looking one step ahead': advice relevant enough to your reality to actually apply. To find your version of Wael:

- Look for someone who has been in your current or next role for the past twelve to twenty-four months.

---

1   See 'Wael Chourbaji', LinkedIn, https://www.linkedin.com/in/wael-chourbaji-88722146/.

- Pick someone in a similar context: the same company, industry or business model.
- Watch how they solve problems, not just what they say.
- Make it a two-way exchange. Share your wins and insights so the relationship grows on both sides.

The biggest barrier to learning? Usually yourself.

Wael helped me see my own patterns. Overthinking simple decisions. Imagining problems that didn't exist. Hesitating when action was better than analysis. 'You're not fighting the system, Sunder. You're fighting yourself,' he once told me.

You can't delegate advocating for yourself. You can't lead with clarity while second-guessing every move. You can't inspire confidence when you're full of doubt. Get out of your own way first. This lesson shaped how I wrote this book.

I'm not a celebrity CEO. I'm someone who has walked your path. Every section in the book should give you something you can use tomorrow, in a meeting, a decision, a tough conversation.

Let's begin with what you can do today.

PART 1
FOUNDATION: Building Your Core Capabilities

VALUES

Volatility Navigation

Volatility Readiness = Foresight + Flexibility + Fast Feedback

In practice: Spot shifts early, adjust without panic and set up quick learning loops so your team can recover faster than competitors.

Anchored in Values

Values-driven Performance = Principles + Pragmatism + Proof

In practice: Anchor trade-offs in non-negotiables, find the path that serves both margins and meaning and let results speak for themselves.

Section 1: Volatility Navigation: Turning Noise into Signals and Speed

At a Glance

When your quarterly plan becomes obsolete by lunch, you need tools that work in chaos.

You'll see how leaders turned disruption into credibility. How they converted ambiguity into action. How they transformed pressure into performance.

Real stories, real solutions, real results.

Along the way, you will learn how:

- I learnt the hard way that perfect plans mean nothing when your top distributors walk away, forcing a leadership pivot I never saw coming.
- Priya broke the optimisation trap and built a flexible lending model that grew 18% while competitors scrambled.
- Arjun turned scenario planning into strategic insurance, cutting launch risk by 40% across Southeast Asia.
- Kavita caught viral trends before headlines. She built an early warning system that unlocked ₹40 crore in fresh revenue streams. Her competition was still reading yesterday's reports.
- You'll master practical tools that work. The Four-Phase Scenario Framework for multiple futures. Knowledge audits that reveal blind spots. Decision-speed tools that beat analysis paralysis.
- To lead through volatility, you need three things: see ahead, stay adaptable, learn fast.

1

The Storm Is the Strategy

You're reviewing quarterly projections when your phone lights up with three news notifications:

- A regulatory change hits 40% of your product portfolio effective next month.
- A competitor launches a product with twice the features at 70% of your price.
- A supply chain disruption halts a key ingredient, now stuck at a port halfway around the world.

By lunch, your carefully crafted strategy feels like yesterday's weather forecast: technically accurate, but no longer useful.

Welcome to middle management. You're juggling delivery and direction. Fielding calls from anxious teams and impatient bosses. Trying to maintain clarity while everything refuses to stay still. You've become the bridge between strategy and execution, even as that bridge sways.

The managers who break through learn to pivot fast, decide with incomplete information and create stability for their teams even when their own ground keeps shifting.

When Planning Fails: A Personal Lesson

In December 2020, I moved to Colombo as the new country GM for Sri Lanka at a global pharmaceutical company. Everything about this role was unfamiliar, since I had never managed a full P&L, never worked in Sri Lanka and never held this title before. Naturally, I did what most new leaders do: I built the perfect plan.

I spent six weeks crafting forty slides of market analysis, competitive positioning and financial projections. Every assumption was pressure-tested with regional heads and veteran GMs. The plan looked bulletproof and I felt ready for everything.

Three months later, two of our largest distributors walked away from the business, taking 20% of our revenue with them. They'd asked for better terms, and when the region said no, they dropped our entire product line without hesitation. My forty-slide deck had no contingency plan for this scenario.

The impact was immediate and painful. Market share dropped 3.5% in a month. Half a month's inventory was there in our warehouse while pharmacies ran empty. Doctors called constantly, frustrated that medications their patients needed were unavailable. Finding new distributors cost eight weeks of lost sales, angry customers and a team losing faith in their new leader.

The moment that stays with me was at a town hall in Colombo when a sales manager who'd been with the company for fifteen years looked at me directly and asked, 'Did you not see this coming?'

He was right. I had not seen it coming. I'd been so focused on building the perfect strategy that I'd forgotten strategies only work when your foundation is stable, and mine wasn't.

That experience taught me something crucial about operating in uncertain environments. Your ability to adapt matters more than your ability to plan. Detailed forecasts make you feel prepared. But when things change quickly, flexibility beats precision. Perfect plans are dangerous comfort zones. The weeks spent perfecting the financial projections would have been better invested in asking practical questions. What happens if a major partner walks away? How quickly can we adjust to currency fluctuations? What's our backup if a product launch gets delayed? These weren't edge cases but predictable vulnerabilities in any volatile market.

The old approach worked when markets moved slowly and competitive advantages lasted. You could update last year's presentation, adjust a few numbers and keep going. That world no longer exists. What makes sense in January might be irrelevant by March.

Planning still matters, but every plan now needs a disclaimer: 'Subject to change without notice.'

Foresight, Flexibility and Fast Feedback: From Prediction to Preparation

The most effective leaders have stopped trying to predict the future perfectly.

They don't build one perfect plan. They prepare for multiple realities. They invest in capabilities that work regardless of which future plays out. They:

- *Build capabilities that transcend scenarios.* Rapid learning, cross-functional team building and data-driven decisions that stay relevant regardless of change.
- *Cultivate early warning systems.* The distributor who shares market gossip. The customer who texts about competitor moves. The supplier who hints at disruptions.
- *Create organisational flexibility.* Teams that pivot fast. People who see change as fuel, not friction. Systems that bend without breaking.

This is the shift from prediction to preparation. The middle managers who rise are early sensors, steady anchors and agile decision-makers who help others navigate the storm. Here's what flexibility, foresight and sensing looks like in action.

Designing for Flexibility: Priya Breaks the Optimisation Trap

Priya led the institutional lending division for a regional bank, managing corporate clients across three states. Her team handled everything, from working capital loans to expansion in financing.

The crisis started when two new digital lenders entered her market, promising loan approvals in hours instead of her team's standard: a week's time. Within three months, four major clients walked away, including a textile manufacturer she had worked with for five years. 'We need working capital decisions in hours, not days,' their CFO told her during their final meeting. 'Your process doesn't match our pace anymore.'

New loan originations dropped 35% that year, and Priya knew she had to act fast.

Her first response was textbook optimisation. She mapped every bottleneck challenge in the approval process, digitised applications and cut required documents from twenty-three to fifteen. She hired two additional analysts and added weekend coverage to speed things up. After three months of intense work, approval time dropped from seven days to three.

Clients kept leaving anyway. One departing customer explained: 'Your process is faster, but it's still rigid. We need partners who adapt to how we work, not the other way around.'

That comment changed Priya's entire approach. She spent the next month studying what the digital lenders offered and discovered the difference wasn't just about the speed but modularity—their systems were configurable, built to change based on what each client needed.

Convincing her leadership team to invest in this new approach took serious political capital. Her proposal to the national head required a complete rethinking of how the bank operated, moving from standardised processes to flexible platforms. The thirty-minute meeting stretched to two hours as they debated what banking relationships mean in a digital world. 'This is a significant shift from everything we've built,' the CFO pointed out.

'Yes,' Priya responded, 'but what we've built is why we're losing.' They approved her plan, though not without reservations.

The redesign went far beyond technology upgrades. Automated pre-screening processed standard applications in four hours. The system could reconfigure itself when regulations changed. Credit analysts now sat with relationship teams, approving loans up to defined thresholds without extra sign-offs.

They also revolutionised their data approach. Historical financial statements gave way to real-time risk assessment. Months-old data became current intelligence. Static reports became dynamic dashboards. But the biggest surprise? They stopped competing with digital lenders and started partnering with them.

Six months later, two events proved the system's value. New environmental regulations hit suddenly. Priya's team adapted in three days. Competitors scrambled for two months. Then clients requested revenue-based repayment instead of fixed monthly payments. Her team prototyped and launched the new product in a week.

Flexibility had become their competitive moat.

The results spoke clearly: the portfolio grew by 18%, existing clients who had threatened to leave stayed and expanded, and several former clients returned. But the deeper change was in how her team thought about their work. They stopped seeing technology as a threat to traditional banking and started seeing change as their competitive advantage.

The shift in thinking was evident in their next client pitch. Instead of highlighting their robust processes, Priya's team emphasised their ability to reconfigure products within days, not months.

Pause and Reflect

In stable environments, efficiency wins. In volatile ones, adaptability is king. This capability signals your readiness for P&L responsibility, where success often hinges on how quickly you can pivot. If you want to step up, stop chasing perfect processes. Build systems that evolve. Favour preparation over perfection, even if it slows things down short term.

- When the next disruption hits, will your systems bend or break?
- Which process looks perfect on paper but would crumble under real pressure?

Flexibility helps you respond faster, but foresight helps you prepare smarter.

Fast Feedback Loops: How Arjun Turned Uncertainty into Learning

Arjun led commercial strategy for a global pharmaceutical company operating across India and Southeast Asia. His MBA had taught him contingency planning, but nothing prepared him for what happened when contingencies themselves needed contingencies.

The regional launch of their new diabetes medication revealed this gap painfully. Indian regulatory approval arrived six months early, but manufacturing delays pushed production for eight weeks. Malaysia changed labelling requirements mid-approval.

Thailand's distributor froze all orders citing market uncertainty. The Philippines demanded additional clinical data which no one had anticipated.

Murphy's Law had become their operating reality.

The team had mapped sixty-five tasks across twelve work streams in their launch plan, a document everyone had praised for its thoroughness; it became useless within weeks. They'd built everything around a single scenario: approvals arriving on schedule, distributors staying committed and supply chains running smoothly. When multiple disruptions hit simultaneously, they had no framework for deciding which fire to fight first.

'Should we delay the entire launch?' leadership asked during an emergency meeting, a question that sent panic through the room.

Arjun knew incremental fixes wouldn't work anymore. At the next steering meeting, he proposed something different: 'Instead of guessing which problem will hit us next, let's prepare for all of them.'

The finance director immediately challenged the approach. 'You're asking for redundancy across every work stream. That's expensive.'

'One month's delay costs us $2 million in lost revenue,' Arjun responded. 'We're buying flexibility, not wasting money on redundancy. Think of this as strategic insurance.'

Over the next quarter, Arjun's team built what they called a multi-path launch system. Backup manufacturing sites stayed at partial readiness. Labels were designed for multiple regulatory scenarios. Shadow launch plans covered adjacent markets. Alternative suppliers were pre-negotiated and ready to go.

Instead of one perfect plan, they had four workable ones. The team identified five forces that could derail any launch. Regulatory timelines started varying by months. Competitor price cuts up to 40%. Supply chain dependencies failing. Currency swings affecting costs. Sudden policy changes like price controls. For each force, they mapped realistic scenarios and tested their responses. The tabletop exercises revealed uncomfortable truths.

One regulatory manager was responsible end to end for four markets across two time zones with no trained backup. When she was on leave, filings stalled and agency queries sat unanswered. There were no pre-negotiated agreements with alternate suppliers. Pricing models were rigid, so the team could not adapt when a competitor moved first. Their very thoroughness had exposed a structural vulnerability. They hired additional regulatory support, signed standby agreements with backup suppliers even at premium rates and created modular pricing structures that could adjust within days rather than weeks.

The real test came sooner than expected. When contamination forced an emergency shutdown of their main manufacturing facility, the backup sites they'd kept partially ready saved them. What could have been a two-month crisis became a five-day adjustment, and the investment in redundancy paid for itself several times over in protected revenue.

But the true validation came through a series of regulatory surprises. Thailand slashed reimbursement rates by 30% without warning. Arjun's team activated pre-designed pricing tiers within seventy-two hours. Competitors spent weeks recalibrating.

Then Malaysia threw them a curveball with new documentation requirements. The team's modular approach allowed them to redirect inventory to the Philippines, turning a potential loss into unexpected revenue.

Flexibility had become profit. The results changed how leadership thought about planning: launch risks dropped by 40%, speed to market improved by 15% and, for the first time on record, they experienced zero stock-outs across the region.

At the regional summit, the business head didn't just praise the results but mandated Arjun's approach for all the product launches.

The transformation was complete. The team had evolved from being excellent at executing plans to being excellent at executing when plans fell apart. That ability to thrive in uncertainty had become their real competitive advantage. In a market where change never stopped, they'd learnt to work with chaos instead of fighting it.

Pause and Reflect

Forecasting assumes tomorrow looks like today. Thinking about potential scenarios prepare for multiple tomorrows. That's the leap middle managers must make, from delivering the plan to protecting value when the plan fails.

- If two major disruptions hit simultaneously tomorrow, what collapses?
- Name your single point of failure. Now, what's your backup?

Sometimes disruption arrives without warning, requiring you to act on incomplete information.

Developing Foresight: Kavita's Early Warning System

Kavita managed regional marketing for a multinational consumer goods company based in Mumbai, with a reputation for spotting trends before competitors noticed them. Last quarter, that ability faced its biggest test.

On a Monday evening, her analytics team flagged unusual social media activity. A beauty influencer with 4 million followers had posted a video criticising their hero skincare product's new formula while praising the older version they'd just discontinued.

By Tuesday morning, the video had 9 million views. By Friday, sales of the reformulated product had dropped by 30%.

The discontinued formula still sitting in warehouses saw demand spike of 150%. Customers hunted for old stock and made bulk orders online. Inventory worth ₹20 crore was suddenly at risk. Retailers cancelled orders for the new formula and demanded the old one back.

The crisis exposed something worse than lost sales: Kavita's forecasting models, built on years of historical data, had completely missed the warning signs. Their quarterly surveys showed nothing alarming; brand tracking indicated steady growth and focus groups had praised the new formula—yet they'd been blindsided by a consumer revolt that had been brewing in online forums for weeks.

Their detection systems were designed to catch trends after they became statistically significant. After thousands of customers had already changed their behaviour. After the damage was done. After prevention was impossible. They'd missed the crucial moment when passionate voices first questioned the reformulation. The narrative had shifted from product effectiveness to ingredient safety before they noticed it. Kavita realised their fundamental error: treating social media as noise rather than a signal. The market had been screaming while they studied spreadsheets. This demanded a complete overhaul.

She built a three-tier detection system over the next two months. Formal tracking: AI-powered sentiment analysis and weekly retailer feedback calls. Informal networks: Monday morning sessions where teams shared warning signals. A collaborative channel for logging anomalies in real time. Rapid response: pre-approved action paths for common scenarios. No committees; no delays; just action.

The investment was modest: social listening tools, CRM upgrades and collaboration platforms cost less than a single failed product launch. Detection was only the beginning as Kavita had to redesign how the entire organisation responded to signals.

Quarterly forecasts became fortnightly updates using real-time data. Manufacturing contracts were renegotiated to allow 30% production swings with ten days' notice. Backup manufacturers stayed on standby. Most importantly, she formed a rapid response team with budget authority and full decision rights. No more committees. No more approval chains. Just speed.

Changing culture turned out harder than fixing operations. The team had to stop fretting over missed predictions and start rewarding fast adaptations. Response time became as important as sales targets in performance reviews.

Six months later, the transformation showed clear results. They launched a clean beauty line in sixteen weeks instead of six months. They captured 15% share in an emerging subcategory by spotting Korean beauty trends early. The combined impact generated ₹40 crore in incremental revenue within the first year.

Speed began translating to revenue.

The real transformation wasn't in the technology or processes; it was in their approach. They stopped asking: 'What just happened?' and started asking: 'What might happen next?' They learnt to distinguish signals from noise at scale. They acted on weak signals before they strengthened.

Sensing and responding to the warning signs had become their competitive advantage in a market where preferences shifted overnight.

Pause and Reflect

Three capabilities separate reactive teams from resilient ones. Spot the signals early, act on it fast and stay clear-headed when surprises land.

- Which weak signals are you dismissing as noise right now?
- When disruption hits, does your team freeze, panic or pivot?

Up Next: The Frameworks That Help Navigate Volatility

Earlier planning assumed predictability. Today's leadership demands adaptability. It's time to shift from reacting to redesigning how you lead through volatility. In the next chapter, we explore decision frameworks that help you act under pressure, when time is short, data is incomplete and choices carry weight.

2

The Volatility Navigator

Most managers freeze when volatility hits because they wait for a level of certainty that never arrives. The ones who move ahead treat volatility navigation as a systematic capability, a set of repeatable routines they can run under pressure. They make sound decisions with incomplete information, commit resources while keeping options open and keep momentum by choosing speed that is safe rather than reckless. This is learnable.

> **Frameworks in this chapter**
>
> **Decision Traffic Lights**
> Purpose: Choose and time decisions by reversibility and impact.
>
> **Confidence Map and Knowledge Gaps**
> Purpose: Separate assumptions from unknowns before you bet.
>
> **The Two-Way Door**
> Purpose: Test high-stakes choices fast, with a clear rollback plan.

Framework 1: Decision Traffic Lights (Choose and time decisions by reversibility and risk)

In volatility, delayed decisions cause more damage than imperfect ones. This framework keeps you from freezing or rushing. Think of it as a traffic light system for decision speed. Every decision gets a track based on reversibility and impact. Here's how it works.

The Three Tracks

Track A: Green Light (two days max.). Can you reverse this decision easily? Move fast.
  These are your daily calls. Pricing adjustments under 5%. Schedule changes. Resource reallocation. One person decides using existing guidelines. Wrong but fast beats right but late.

Track B: Yellow Light (five days max.). Will this affect the current quarter? Move carefully.
  Distribution partner changes. Launch timing adjustments. Vendor switches. Quick consultation with key stakeholders. Two approvals maximum. Speed with input, not committees.

Track C: Red Light (seven days max.). Will impact last beyond this year? Move deliberately.
  Days 1–2: Frame the real problem, not symptoms.
  Days 3–4: Gather only decision-critical data.
  Days 5–6: Model three scenarios maximum.
  Day 7: Decide and communicate.
  Structure keeps panic at bay and decisions moving.

Quick Test

Three questions sort any decision:

- Easily reversible? → Track A
- Quarter-only impact? → Track B
- Year-plus consequences? → Track C

Warning Signs

You're misusing this framework if:

- Green decisions need multiple meetings
- Yellow decisions involve more than five people
- Red decisions extend past seven days

The most common failure? Everything becomes Track C because that feels safest.

These timeframes are starting points, not laws. A start-up might compress them by half. A regulated industry might need double for compliance. What matters is having clear categories that your team understands.

Most importantly, teams learn to distinguish data that informs from data that merely confirms. They build confidence in their ability to act decisively without perfect information.

The Timing Paradox: A Personal Lesson

Most of the time you win by moving at a safe speed. But every so often the highest-leverage move is to wait. That is not indecision but a deliberate choice to align context before you commit. Organisational timing can matter more than individual readiness because some decisions depend on the right audience, the right sponsor or the right sequence of events.

In June 2016, I joined the India affiliate of a global pharmaceutical company as general manager of sales and marketing excellence, responsible for driving execution across our

4,000-person salesforce. Like most new leaders, I arrived with ideas to prove my value quickly. Mine was a machine learning platform that could coach sales reps and sharpen their messaging. The pilot results were compelling: sales productivity jumped 23% across six test territories. I spent weeks perfecting the business case, gathering field manager support, and securing our tech partner's commitment. This wasn't just an India opportunity; it could scale globally.

In November, I walked into Rajeev Barataria's office, the executive VP for commercial, with my forty-five-minute presentation ready. He listened without interrupting, asked a few pointed questions, then said, 'Great idea, Sunder. Truly innovative. But now is not the right time.'

Stunned, I asked, 'The results are obvious. Why wait?'

His answer was a lesson in organisational dynamics. The regional APAC head had just left, with a replacement arriving in three weeks. During leadership transitions, bold initiatives from local markets get killed not on merit but on timing. His hardest instruction: 'Don't share this idea with anyone. Not regional IT, not your peers. Sit on it for three months.'

I walked out frustrated, wondering if Rajeev was being overly cautious or simply didn't understand the opportunity. But Rajeev had spent thirty-five years navigating corporate systems and understood something I didn't. In corporate life, timing often beats brilliance.

Three months later, he called to say the global commercial head was visiting and I'd have twenty minutes. With additional data and refined positioning, I pitched again. The global head authorised immediate regional rollout. Within a year, the platform deployed across Asia-Pacific, then Latin America, then parts of the US. An idea that could have died in a leadership transition became a global success.

When I thanked Rajeev later, he shared something I've never forgotten: 'In volatility, everyone wants to move fast. Sometimes the smartest strategy is patience. Wait for the right audience and context. Let the organisation become ready for your idea.'

That changed how I approach decisions. Now I ask not just 'How should we move?' but 'Should we move now?', because moving fast doesn't help if the moment isn't right.

Framework 2: Confidence Map and Knowledge Gaps (Separate assumptions from unknowns before you bet)

Perfect information is a luxury volatile markets don't offer. The managers who advance don't pretend to know everything. They systematically identify what they need to know, what they can live without and which signals reveal breaking assumptions. A knowledge audit makes uncertainty visible and actionable.

Step 1: Map Critical Assumptions

List the beliefs your strategy depends on. This is your Confidence Map. Assign confidence levels based on evidence, not optimism.

When launching in a new market, for example, these might be some assumptions:

- Regulatory timeline will hold (80% confidence)
- Competitors won't accelerate (60% confidence)
- Supply chain handles surge (70% confidence)
- Customers pay without insurance (45% confidence)

That 45% confidence should trigger immediate preventive action. Alternative pricing models. Phased entry. Additional research. The power comes from making assumptions explicit and debatable.

Teams often discover that their most critical assumptions have the lowest confidence.

Step 2: Identify Knowledge Gaps That Matter

Not all uncertainty deserves investigation. Filter ruthlessly. The key question is: will this information change our approach? Can we get it in time? Is it worth the effort? Focus on gaps that alter decisions, not satisfy curiosity.

Step 3: Build Early Warning Systems

For each critical assumption, establish signals that indicate it's proving to be incorrect.

- *Quantitative triggers*: 20% variance in metrics. Complaints exceeding thresholds. Supplier delays beyond limits.
- *Qualitative triggers*: Multiple sources raising similar concerns. Sentiment shifts lasting two weeks. Unusual competitor patterns.

The key is to recognise patterns before they strengthen. Create weekly 'anomaly sessions' where teams share odd observations without judgement. Strange customer requests. Unexpected competitor moves. Unusual supplier behaviour. Today's dismissed oddity might explain next week's crisis.

These thresholds are starting points. Your context determines whether 20% or 5% variance matters. Whether you need weekly or daily reviews. What's essential is having triggers before you need them.

Winners spot shifts before the numbers reflect them.

Framework 3: The Two-Way Door (Test, hedge, or reverse decisions quickly)

In volatile markets, agility beats precision. This framework helps you stay bold while keeping room to adjust. Amazon calls it designing 'two-way doors' instead of 'one-way doors' you can't exit. The goal is to keep moving without mistaking hesitation for caution.

The framework works across three levels of reversibility. Each level gives you different ways to preserve flexibility while still making progress. Think of these as your toolkit for decision-making under uncertainty, from fully reversible choices to strategic hedging.

The Three Levels

Level 1: Fully reversible. These decisions can be reversed completely with minimal cost.

Example: Pilot an idea in one location/unit before going system-wide. Use month-to-month contracts instead of annual locks. Run proofs-of-concept before full implementation.

You get maximum learning with minimum lock-in.

Level 2: Modifiable. These can be adjusted significantly but not fully reversed.

Example: Modular systems where components can be swapped out. Phased investments with clear stage-gates. Platforms with strong integration capabilities.

You are designing pivot points so you can change direction on real signals rather than tearing down and starting over.

Level 3: Not easily reversible.

When the choice is hard to unwind, create parallel paths to protect the outcome. For example, keep three suppliers instead of one. Pay a small premium for contracts that allow quantity or feature changes. Staff volatile projects with a higher share of generalists. Maintain a warm alternative even after you pick a primary option. A small insurance premium beats having to rebuild from scratch.

Where to Apply Reversibility

The key is knowing where to build flexibility into your decisions.

For market entry: start with one city, not five. For technology: choose open systems over closed. For teams: build versatility over specialisation.

The trade is always the same: a bit of speed for a lot more resilience.

Use this approach when:

- Signals are contradictory
- Multiple futures seem equally likely
- Being wrong costs more than being flexible
- Speed beats optimisation
- External factors could force changes

The trade-off: Flexibility costs 5–15% more initially. But when disruption hits, your modular system reconfigures in days while competitors need months. Your redundant suppliers keep you running when others stop. That small premium is what buys your edge.[1]

---

1 Jeff Bezos, '2015 Letter to Shareholders. Amazon.com, Inc', Sec. gov, 2015, https:/www.sec.gov/Archives/edgar/ data/1018724/ 000119312516530910/d168744dex991.htm.

Avoiding the Common Volatility Traps

Three mistakes trip up even sharp managers in volatile times. Avoid them by building systematic learning and decision routines.

- *The hero complex*: Solving every crisis personally rather than building systems. Senior leaders don't want firefighters but architects whose designs prevent fires.
- *Analysis paralysis*: Confusing thorough analysis with good judgement. In volatility, a good decision today beats a perfect decision next month.
- *Rigidity reflex*: Responding to uncertainty by creating more rules and processes. This signals fear, not leadership. Volatility requires flexible principles, not rigid rules.

Treat every decision as a learning opportunity, not just execution. Run after-action reviews within two weeks of major decisions. Document what you expected versus what happened and what you'll do differently. Keep these sessions blame-free and learning-focused.

Document lessons systematically. Create decision journals capturing context, logic and outcomes. Build pattern libraries of recurring challenges. Share stories across the organisation. These actions transform individual learning into organisational capability.

Signalling Leadership Readiness

Senior leaders evaluating you for advancement look for specific volatility capabilities. They watch whether you freeze or adapt when crises converge. Whether you make decisive calls despite incomplete information. Whether you create stability for others while navigating your own uncertainty.

The evaluation goes beyond crisis response. Do you build systems that anticipate disruption, not just react? Do you spot weak signals before they become threats? Can you maintain strategic clarity when operational chaos demands all your attention?

These capabilities signal readiness for ambiguity. Most critically, they observe your judgement under pressure. Which decisions need speed versus deliberation? Can you commit resources while maintaining flexibility? Do you turn disruption into advantage rather than panic?

Volatility will either stretch you or stop you.

3

View from the Top with Rajiv Jayaraman

To understand what volatility navigation looks like from the top, I asked Rajiv Jayaraman, co-founder and CEO of KNOLSKAPE, a leader in experiential learning technology.[1] *When COVID hit, almost 60–70% of his company's revenue vanished overnight. Rajiv saw first-hand which managers could navigate true uncertainty. His career has been spent helping organisations prepare for disruption and he has faced his own crucible moment.*

Here's what he had to say.

Leading Through Volatility

In times of stability, management can feel like steering a steady ship. But in volatility, leadership becomes less about direction and more about navigation. Mid-managers sit at the crucial intersection of strategy and execution, where uncertainty hits hardest and clarity is most demanded.

I experienced this during the Covid-19 crisis. KNOLSKAPE focuses on experiential learning tech for organisational and leadership development. Almost 60–70% of our revenues were wiped out overnight. Our entire business model relied heavily on

---

1 See 'Rajiv Jayaraman', LinkedIn, https://www.linkedin.com/in/rajivjayaraman/.

in-person experiences and suddenly became irrelevant. It was a moment of truth.

In such situations, there's no playbook, only principles. The two anchors that kept us from capsizing were culture and trust. Because we had built a culture of psychological safety and purpose, our teams came together instinctively. Not out of fear, but out of shared ownership.

What I Saw in Our Managers

Certain mid-managers at KNOLSKAPE emerged as true force multipliers during this period. They didn't just execute instructions. They reimagined problems, connected dots across functions and created new opportunities where none existed.

We pivoted rapidly to a 100% online delivery model and leveraged our core strengths of being tech-first. This wouldn't have been possible without the resilience of our managers. Their resilience wasn't blind optimism. It was grounded in systems thinking and the understanding that volatility is not chaos but the byproduct of interdependent systems shifting simultaneously.

As Nassim Nicholas Taleb reminds us in his book *Fooled by Randomness*, 'We tend to mistake noise for signal.' The best managers resisted that temptation. They paused to separate transient fluctuations from structural changes, enabling smarter, more sustainable responses.

Systems Thinking in Action

Systems thinking helps mid-managers see beyond the immediate challenges. It teaches them to zoom out, to understand how actions in one part of the system ripple through the whole.

When revenue lines were collapsing, some of our managers didn't just ask, 'How do we cut costs?' Rather, they asked, 'How might we reconfigure value?' This shift in perspective led to new digital offerings, hybrid models and ways of engaging clients we hadn't considered before.

Resilience and creative problem-solving are often romanticised, but in practice, they're deeply systemic. Resilience is not endurance. It's adaptation. Creativity is not a flash of inspiration. It's the outcome of connecting disparate elements in new ways.

The managers who thrived built micro-systems of learning, feedback and experimentation. Small loops that kept the organisation agile.

What This Means for Mid-Managers

In an age where randomness can upend entire industries overnight, mid-managers must learn to be translators of volatility. Turning noise into narrative. Disruption into design. They need to think in systems, act with empathy and create spaces where teams can cohere around purpose even when the future is blurry.

Volatility isn't going away. But organisations don't rise or fall with markets alone. They do so with the quality of thinking and connection within their middle layers. The future belongs to those who can hold both the big picture and the human picture together.

4

Do-It Notes: Your Volatility Navigation Road Map

Now it's time to convert volatility insights into systematic practice. The core question isn't 'How do I survive disruption?' but 'How do I architect decision systems that turn volatility into competitive advantage before others see the shift?'

Reflect Before You Act

'Plans are useless, but planning is indispensable.'

—Dwight D. Eisenhower

Do-It Notes

This Month: Diagnose and Build Foundation

1. *Map your decision flow.* Track every significant decision for two weeks. Identify where analysis paralysis hits and where you move too fast. Find the bottlenecks that everyone pretends don't exist.
2. *Tap your early trend-spotters.* Identify three sharp observers. Your most demanding customer. The supplier who knows

everyone. The peer who navigated this successfully. Ask each one of them, 'What patterns are you seeing that I'm missing?'
3. *Challenge one critical assumption.* Pick your highest-stakes belief about current strategy. Rate your confidence from 1–10. List three ways you could be catastrophically wrong. Share these points with your team and watch them battle with them.
4. *Pilot your decision charter.* Define your green/yellow/red decision tiers. Set clear criteria. Run a two-week test. Track where the structure breaks, then fix it.

This Quarter: Build Your Response Systems

1. *Establish your sensing routine.* Launch 'Weak Signal Wednesdays'. Spend fifteen minutes weekly surfacing anomalies. Odd customer requests. Strange competitor moves. Unusual supplier delays. Log everything, dismiss nothing.
2. *Run one scenario simulation.* Pick three nightmares that keep you awake. Where would your strategy crack? Run a tabletop simulation based on a past disaster. Make a note of what you're not ready for.
3. *Build your volatility dashboard.* Select three to five metrics that give thirty- to sixty-day warnings. Choose specific metrics such as customer sentiment (CSAT or NPS), supplier lead time (PO to delivery) and a competitor price index (weighted basket), then set yellow and red thresholds and review them weekly. Act on the yellow decision tier before it turns red.
4. *Design one reversible initiative.* Apply Framework 3 to your next project. Build in explicit pivot points. Define triggers for course changes. Maintain warm alternatives.

This Year: Demonstrate Enterprise Thinking

1. *Embed scenario thinking everywhere.* Every strategic proposal should show multiple futures. Every plan should demonstrate resilience when assumptions break. Make this your signature move.
2. *Create your volatility reserve.* Keep 10% of the budget flexible. For rapid pivots. For backup vendors. For sudden opportunities. Log every instance where speed delivered value.
3. *Build your leadership portfolio.* Document three specific wins:
    - You spotted a shift before others saw it
    - You made a fast call that prevented disaster
    - You turned volatility into competitive advantage.

    Structure these as case studies for performance reviews and promotion conversations.

The Non-Negotiables

Commit to three practices that compound:

- *Daily*: The decision log (fifteen minutes). Record what you decided, how long it took, and what happened next.
- *Weekly*: The weak-signals session (thirty minutes). Ask each team member to flag anomalies they have noticed and put them on record. No judgement at this stage, only observation and brief context.
- *Quarterly*: The scenario review (two hours). Test your current strategy against likely disruptions and adjust plans where the assumptions no longer hold.

Do-It Notes: Your Volatility Navigation Road Map 33

You'll know it's working when:

- Decisions that took weeks now take days
- Your team spots issues before they become crises
- Surprises (uncertainty) decrease while preparedness increases
- Others ask how you 'saw that coming'
- Volatility becomes opportunity, not threat

Up Next

But the next test is trickier. Performance pressures will collide with your values. Trade-offs will get personal. How do you lead when doing right might cost you everything?

That's where we're headed next.

Section 2: Anchored in Values: Making Values a Competitive Advantage

At a Glance

In scenarios where values clash with quarterly targets, managers who advance learn to build something stronger from the tension rather than seeing only compromise. That mindset is the foundation of principled leadership, which treats values as operating guidance for hard choices. This section shows how principled leadership, when practised with clarity and courage, becomes a competitive strength.

Along the way, you will learn how:

- I faced a value versus viability dilemma during Sri Lanka's economic crisis and learnt that values mean solving harder problems with greater responsibility, not compromising on business.
- Priya turned environmental scrutiny into stakeholder trust and ₹30 crore in new business by refusing to compromise and inventing a better path.
- Arjun invested ₹75 lakh in quality standards that his team called unnecessary until those very standards became the reason a multinational awarded his manufacturing site ₹120 crore in supply contracts.
- Kavita chose costly reformulation over profitable status quo when early signals questioned product safety.

You can apply three practical frameworks: the Reality Check Protocol to audit your operative values, the Values Radar to spot ethical flashpoints early and the Five Gates to navigate values decisions systematically. Use the Do-It Notes to embed values into systems, decisions and culture.

To lead with values, you need to act on what matters, find practical ways to deliver and show results that earn trust.

5
When Values Get Tested

Your biggest client calls asking you to cut corners on quality standards to meet their Monday morning deadline. The contract is worth ₹15 crore, enough to secure team bonuses and hit your division's annual growth target. You have twenty-four hours to decide. This is a classic example of when values leadership stops being theoretical.

'It Boils Down to You'—A Personal Lesson

In April 2022, when I was country GM in Sri Lanka, we discovered a labelling error on a popular paediatric cough syrup. The infant version carried dosing information meant for older children—potentially dangerous if followed.

The business case for a quiet fix was compelling. Many parents don't pay enough attention to labels. Doctors knew the correct dosing. We were in Sri Lanka's worst economic crisis, and a product recall would create panic while costing significant money. We could correct future labels and let existing stock sell through. I was tempted.

I shared this dilemma with Dr Chatura Jayakody,[1] our medical affairs head. His response cut through my commercial calculus:

---

1   See 'Chatura Jayakody', LinkedIn, https://linkedin.com/in/dr-chatura-jayakody-99b21262/.

'You're thinking like a commercial leader, Sunder. Think like a father whose child might take this medicine. The question is not whether you can afford to be wrong; it is whether you can accept looking wrong in the short term for doing what is right, because a recall in the middle of a national crisis can look like overreaction or poor control and it will hurt the quarter, yet it is the action that prevents harm. The lens you choose shapes your decision. It finally boils down to you.'

That reframed everything. The risk wasn't just regulatory fines or reputation damage. It was a parent giving their sick infant the wrong dose. One adverse event would destroy more than trust. I thought to myself, if this gets discovered then the headline would be: 'Pharma Giant Knew of Labelling Error, Stayed Silent.'

But the deeper cost would be living with the knowledge that we chose business continuity over children's safety.

We recalled every bottle from every shelf. The next ten weeks tested every principle we claimed to hold as we managed regulatory questions, distributor complaints and significant financial loss. There was no path that preserved both safety and secrecy, but there was never really a choice, not when you framed the situation correctly.

This experience taught me that values don't live in mission statements or company posters. They reveal themselves in moments when easier paths exist, when justifications are readily available. When pressure mounts and stakes rise, the lens you choose determines the outcome.

There's another benefit most people don't discuss. Values make decision-making simpler. When fairness, transparency and safety are non-negotiable, you don't second-guess them every quarter. Grey areas disappear. Decisions accelerate. Clarity becomes your competitive advantage.

Every middle manager encounters moments when the easier path beckons, when you feel tempted to overlook concerning data, accept 'good enough' standards, dismiss early warnings as noise. These are the moments that define careers.

Priya, Arjun and Kavita each stood at similar crossroads and found ways to turn ethical dilemmas into business advantages.

When Integrity Demands Innovation: Priya's Banking Crisis

One year after launching her flexible lending platform, Priya faced her first real test as head of institutional lending when her biggest client, a manufacturing conglomerate generating ₹20 crore yearly in fees, needed emergency financing for a project in Odisha. Routine enough, until her due diligence team flagged serious concerns: potential groundwater contamination and displacement of fishing communities along the river.

That evening's virtual meeting was tense. The client's CFO was direct: 'We've been with your bank for eight years. We're not asking you to break laws, just fast-track this based on our internal assessments. Every other bank is ready to move. Don't make us rethink this relationship.'

The threat was clear: losing them meant missing targets, team bonuses and possibly her promotion.

The next morning, her manager cornered her: 'We can't afford to lose this client because of some environmental issues. Make it work.'

Most people would have seen two choices: compromise integrity or lose the client. Priya found a third way. Over the weekend she reframed the problem. Instead of asking how to push the loan through, she asked how to finance it in a way that turns compliance into value by protecting the bank's capital and reputation while allowing the project to proceed only if it meets objective environmental and community tests. The goal was not to manage the project on the client's behalf or to chase fees at any cost, but to lend against lawful milestones that reduce loss risk and avoid franchise damage.

She proposed a three-tranche structure that linked disbursement to verified safeguards. Tranche one would follow submission of statutory environmental clearances and a baseline water monitoring plan verified by an independent assessor. Tranche two would require signed community compensation and resettlement agreements placed in escrow, along with evidence of local grievance redress. Tranche three would be contingent on a third-party audit ninety days into construction confirming that groundwater thresholds and discharge norms remained within the approved limits. Each tranche included suspension triggers and step-down rights so the bank could pause exposure if a condition failed, which meant fees would come from lawful activity and returns would be tied to de-risked progress rather than optimistic projections.

This was not idealism; it was risk management that priced integrity into the structure.

Her team worked through the weekend building the model. First tranche: land and permits only. Second tranche: verified environmental assessments and community compensation. Final funding: all approvals secured and documented. Risk management presented through compliance.

Her manager called it expensive handholding and the client resisted at first. Priya brought data. Three similar projects in neighbouring districts had stalled after investing ₹50 crore each, not because protests were preventable by a bank, but because the social risk was foreseeable and never priced or staged into the financing. Her structure and due diligence would highlight that risk early, limit exposure if conditions failed and protect capital while enabling execution. It was strategic insurance.

Three months later, everything changed. The environmental assessment revealed an alternative site layout that avoided the water table and saved ₹2 crore in foundation costs. Early community engagement reduced the likelihood of the disruptions that had plagued competitors. The project finished ahead of schedule. Compliance had become competitive advantage.

The client brought Priya into expansion planning across three states. They introduced her to two other corporations facing similar challenges. Result: ₹30 crore in new business. All built on that first difficult stand.

Her manager named this function 'intelligent stakeholder management' and used it as a case study for the region.

Pause and Reflect

Values-based leadership means redesigning challenges so that integrity drives profitability, not having to choose between the two.

- When pressured to compromise, do you retreat, comply or redesign?
- Which 'constraint' in your role is actually an untapped advantage?

Sometimes the pressure comes from colleagues who think you're holding standards unreasonably high.

Arjun's Quality Gamble: When the Team Pushes Back

When the audit report landed on Arjun's desk, he knew he had a crisis on his hands. Their diabetes medication supplier was using raw materials that technically passed regulations but skirted quality boundaries. The active ingredient met minimum purity standards but contained trace impurities at the upper limits of acceptability. These findings had slipped past internal checks for months.

Arjun faced brutal choices. Stay with the supplier and risk patient safety. Switch suppliers and face 20% higher costs plus an eight-week supply gap. Halt production and leave patients without medication. He saw a fourth path: build in-house quality testing beyond industry norms, partnering with three certified suppliers instead of just one to prevent future dependencies.

His leadership team revolted immediately. 'You're over-engineering a non-issue,' his production head argued during a heated meeting. 'The supplier passed inspection. This is pharma, not aerospace.'

The finance director was equally critical: 'Corporate will react strongly when they see this. You're proposing a 20% margin hit plus ₹75 lakh in capital expenditure for a problem that doesn't technically exist.'

Arjun spent the weekend building his case, positioning enhanced quality as strategic risk mitigation rather than operational expense. Regional leadership approved reluctantly, giving him six months to prove the value of his proposal.

Implementation was painful. Equipment vendors missed deadlines. New testing protocols required triple validation. Certified suppliers knew they had leverage and negotiated accordingly. They missed the pre-monsoon launch window, delaying ₹5 crore in revenue.

'You're solving hypothetical problems with real money,' his boss warned during a tense review. Arjun held firm: 'What looks hypothetical today becomes headline news tomorrow, and by then it's too late.'

Six months later, the headline arrived: 'Major Pharma Recall: Contaminated Diabetes Drug Affects 50,000 Patients.' A competitor using the same raw material supplier had fallen for the trap they had narrowly avoided. They were now facing regulatory investigations, patient lawsuits and stock price collapse. Arjun's gamble had become foresight.

Within weeks, three major hospital chains switched to Arjun's company. They specifically cited 'beyond-compliance quality protocols' for the switch. Orders jumped 40%.

But the real validation came when a global pharma major spent two days auditing their facilities. 'Most sites meet standards,' their head of operations noted. 'Yours exceeds them. That's the difference between a vendor and a partner.' And they signed the partnership agreement. The contract brought ₹120 crore over three years.

The ₹75 lakh investment transformed more than finances. The site's culture evolved from accepting what was 'good enough' to thinking at every stage 'what could go wrong?' Teams spotted risks others missed. They designed for problems that hadn't yet materialised. When global standards tightened two years later, they were ready while competitors scrambled to keep up.

Pause and Reflect

Standards you raise only when forced aren't standards. They're compliance. Real standards hold especially when no one's watching. They cost something upfront. But they become your competitive moat when others cut corners.

- What standards does your team resist because 'good enough' seems fine today?
- When facing internal pushback, do you back down, argue harder or demonstrate future value?

Sometimes the hardest resistance comes from colleagues who dismiss ethical choices as performative rather than practical.

Kavita's Green Gamble: When Marketing Called It 'Virtue Signalling'

Three beauty bloggers with 5 million followers combined had started targeting Kavita's bestselling personal care line with a consistent message that these ingredients were toxic.

The line generated ₹200 crore annually, representing 35% of portfolio sales. The ingredients were legal, approved, industry-standard. But Kavita's early warning system was picking up converging signals. Dermatologists reported rising sensitivity complaints. Customer service noted ingredient questions spiking. Trend analysts flagged clean beauty moving mainstream. The pattern was unmistakable.

The numbers were brutal. They had ₹80 crore of existing inventory with twelve-month shelf life. Reformulation meant writing off ₹30 crore of stock, plus ₹5 crore in development costs, four months of lost sales and a 15% price increase that could eliminate their mass-market position.

'We're looking at a ₹50 crore hit to address concerns that aren't scientifically proven,' the CFO calculated. 'These ingredients have been safe for forty years.' Her marketing director was blunter: 'We're destroying a profitable product because 2% of the market is making noise? This is expensive virtue signalling.'

Kavita had tracked consumer trends for fifteen years and recognised the pattern. Fringe concern becomes influencer adoption. Influencer adoption becomes mainstream demand. Mainstream demand becomes regulatory action. What once took five years now happened in eighteen months.

The data confirmed her instinct: premium retail growing 3x faster than mass market, millennial clean product spending up 30% yearly, competitors' natural brands showing 45% growth.

Her teenaged nephew had stopped using the product after researching ingredients online. When Kavita asked why, he said simply, 'Would you put something on your skin if you weren't sure it was safe?'

That question crystallised her decision. The company claimed 'Consumer Trust Above All' as its core value, yet here was Kavita selling something she wouldn't confidently recommend to her own family. She made the call to reformulate immediately despite the financial tension ahead.

The execution was brutal. They had to sell existing inventory while developing new formulas, creating a dangerous perception gap. Sales teams felt demoralised pushing products the company was simultaneously replacing. Retailers demanded steep discounts to clear old stock. The transition stretched from four to seven months when new formulas failed stability tests. Quarter after quarter, Kavita faced hostile reviews. 'You've destroyed our most profitable line based on Instagram hysteria,' became the recurring accusation.

Ten months later, a major study linked the questioned ingredients to hormone disruption. What seemed like overreaction suddenly looked like prescient leadership. Competitors scrambled to reformulate under regulatory pressure and public backlash. Kavita's brand was already established in the clean beauty market.

The results validated every difficult decision: 30% market share in clean beauty; ₹200 crore revenue within eighteen months; restored consumer trust. The new line commanded a 15% premium and opened previously closed retail channels.

Virtue signalling had become market leadership. The transformation went beyond products. Her team learnt to treat weak signals as early indicators, not noise. Their early warning system became an early action system. They stopped chasing shifts and started leading them.

Pause and Reflect

Values aren't values if you only follow them when the data is conclusive and the path is profitable.

- When facing weak signals that challenge profitable products, do you wait for proof or act on conviction?
- Can you hold firm when everyone thinks you're overreacting?

Up Next: The Frameworks to Scale Values with Systems

You've seen how integrity drives innovation, earns trust and builds resilience. But how do you embed that into daily operations? How do you make values systematic, not heroic?

In the next chapter, we'll break down practical frameworks to stress-test decisions, coach teams and build cultures where doing the right thing is just how business gets done.

6
The Values Edge

Most managers treat values dilemmas as unavoidable conflicts between doing right and doing well. The leaders who advance understand something different: values are a systematic capability. You sense ethical flashpoints before they explode, close gaps between stated and operative values and transform constraints into opportunities.

> **Frameworks in this chapter**
>
> **The Reality Check Protocol**
> Purpose: Show how values actually drive decisions under pressure and trade-offs.
>
> **The Values Radar**
> Purpose: Spot ethical flashpoints early and set simple triggers to act.
>
> **Five Gates**
> Purpose: Five questions every major decision must pass before approval.

Framework 1: The Reality Check Protocol (How values actually drive decisions in your organisation)

Most companies display 'Integrity' and 'Excellence' in reception areas. But when your biggest customer demands shortcuts and your boss says, 'Just make the numbers,' those values become buzzwords. This framework reveals what actually drives decisions versus what gets proclaimed in town halls. That truth usually stings a little. As a middle manager, you're auditing your sphere of influence, including your team, department and key stakeholders.

Step 1: Audit Your Operative Values

Document three recent high-stakes decisions. Compare what should have driven the choice with what actually did. The gap reveals your starting point for changing how decisions are made and what gets rewarded.

Look for pattern in decisions, incentives and consequences:

- What behaviours got people promoted in the last eighteen months?
- When there was a conflict between speed and quality, which was given precedence?
- Which shortcuts were quietly tolerated when targets are at risk?

If everyone promoted chooses speed over thoroughness, if quality issues disappear when deadlines loom, then 'speed' is your operative value.

Step 2: Name Your Real Values

Once you've identified patterns, name them honestly. For example,

- A pharmaceutical team may discover 'patient safety above margins'
- A technology team may realise 'user privacy over feature speed'
- A financial services team may value 'relationships over quick wins'

Use these named values as filters for real decisions. Apply them at three gates: when you plan (what you will and will not do), when you budget (what gets funded or deferred) and when you escalate (what you will defend if challenged)

Step 3: Close the Gap

You can't change the entire organisation. But you can influence your domain.

- *With your team*: Make real values explicit. Recognise those who act on them despite pressure. Frame this change as leadership development.
- *With your boss*: Translate values into business language. Not 'this is right' but 'this reduces risk by X%' or 'this protects customer lifetime value'.

Values survive only when they make business sense.

Making it work: Audit annually. Track whether gaps are being closed. Document instances where values-based decisions led to measurable outcomes. This becomes your evidence of cultural transformation and your case for advancement.

Framework 2: Values Radar (Spot ethical flashpoints before they flare up)

Values get tested when money and morals collide. This framework helps you spot collisions for six to twelve months before they become crises. Catching such issues early turns values conflicts into opportunities.

Step 1: Map Vulnerability Zones

Identify the common situations in your industry where business pressure and values collide:

- *Regulation:* Rules that are tightening or likely to tighten. New environmental limits may make current processes non-compliant, and safety requirements may raise the minimum standard beyond what teams use today. Compliance changes can alter core operations.
- *Social licence:* Issues that can trigger public or employee backlash before regulators act, such as transparency on sourcing, community impact or fair treatment of contractors.
- *Technology:* Changes that introduce ethical dilemmas, such as AI that replaces human judgement, automation that affects employment or features that create privacy risk.

List five to seven zones that matter to your business. Score each on likelihood and business impact, then select three priority zones. These are the ones you will monitor and escalate first.

Step 2: Build Your Sensing Network

Create listening posts across formal and informal channels.

- *Formal signals (6–12 months warning)*: Regulatory consultation papers, which focus on what's being discussed but isn't yet mandated. Academic research that challenges existing practices. Industry agendas shifting priorities.
- *Informal signals (3–6 months warning)*: Frontline concerns during coffee conversations. Supplier nervousness about existing practices. Competitors hiring ethics officers.

When three unconnected sources flag similar concerns within a month, investigate immediately.

Step 3: Convert to Advantage

Turn early warnings into moves others do not see coming. Start by deciding whether a cue is noise or a signal. Treat it as a signal when it repeats across at least two independent sources over two weeks, affects a priority customer or regulator or shows rising frequency or severity. Then judge whose concern carries weight with a simple rubric:

- *Source credibility*: First-hand data and direct observation outrank opinion.
- *Exposure to consequences:* People who bear the cost if it goes wrong outrank bystanders.
- *Decision rights:* Regulators, top customers and critical suppliers outrank internal commentators.
- *Scope:* Issues that span multiple teams or markets outrank local irritants. If two or more criteria score high, escalate.

Then calculate the cost of acting now versus being caught unprepared.

Finally, design moves that turn constraints into capabilities. If customers question ingredients, reformulate before regulations force you. If employees flag safety concerns, upgrade before accidents occur. If stakeholders want transparency, disclose before scrutiny demands it.

Making It Work: These timeframes are starting points. Your industry determines whether you need monthly or quarterly analysis.

Start with one vulnerability zone. Monitor thoroughly. Expand once that works. Document where early detection created opportunities. That's your business case for continued investment in sensing systems.

Framework 3: Five Gates (Five questions every major decision must pass)

When values and performance clash, gut instinct isn't enough. Every decision either builds or erodes trust. This framework transforms ethical dilemmas into strategic decisions.

These five questions slow you down, preventing pressure from scrambling judgement.

The Five Questions

Question 1: What are the real stakes?

An investment in quality systems might delay this quarter's profits but secure three years of premium contracts. Document both.

Map immediate and long-term costs.

- *Hard costs*: revenue, margins, operations
- *Soft costs*: trust, reputation, morale
- *Hidden costs*: future opportunities, talent retention

Question 2: Who's affected beyond the obvious?

When cutting corners, remember employees normalise shortcuts, while suppliers question standards.
Look past immediate stakeholders.

- *Direct impact*: customers, employees, shareholders
- *Secondary*: suppliers, partners, communities
- *Future*: potential clients watching your reliability

Question 3: Does it pass the front-page test?

- Would this survive public scrutiny?
- Could you defend this in a media interview? Explain it to regulators without hedging? Stay comfortable if all details surfaced?

If you're hoping aspects stay hidden, you have your answer.

Question 4: Is there a third way?

Reject binary thinking. Not environment *or* client relationships; restructure deals so that compliance adds value. Not quality *or* costs; redesign for both safety and efficiency. Not speed *or* thoroughness; create staged approaches.
False dilemmas trick you into bad choices.

Question 5: What precedent does this decision set?

Cultural impact outlasts financial impact.

- Every decision quietly teaches what really counts.

- Will this action encourage transparency or precipitate hidden crises?
- Will this signal that principles bend or hold?
- Will this be model behaviour that others will copy?

Making It Work: Don't rely on memory under pressure. Build these into infrastructure. Add all five questions as required fields in templates. Rotate a devil's advocate's role in meetings. Journal which questions change your decisions the most; those are blind spots.

Time pressure shortcut: use Question 3 alone. The front-page test catches most ethical missteps.

Common Pitfalls in Values-Based Leadership

Three traps consistently derail managers trying to lead with values:

Analysis Paralysis: Faced with a values dilemma, some managers keep collecting data, seeking more opinions and waiting for a risk-free option that never appears. The search for certainty becomes the excuse for delay. Values decisions rarely offer perfect clarity, so the better standard is a timely, defensible choice that protects people, meets the policy and law, and can be explained with evidence and intent.

Progress requires moving forward with your best judgement, then adjusting as you learn.

The Martyr Complex: Others turn values into theatrics, broadcasting their suffering at every opportunity. They frame every ethical choice as sacrifice. Every standard becomes a burden. Every decision requires a team. This backfires spectacularly.

Values start looking like luxuries the business can't afford. The managers who advance frame values differently. Higher standards attract better talent. Transparency accelerates decisions. Trust reduces transaction costs. They don't talk about what they're giving up. They demonstrate what they're gaining

The Isolation Error: The costliest mistake: Trying to be your organisation's sole conscience. These managers exhaust themselves fighting alone. They become cynical when they fail, self-righteous when they succeed. Neither outcome helps anyone.

Sustainable values-based leadership requires allies, not martyrdom. The finance leader worried about penalties becomes your compliance partner. The operations head who has seen quality damage relationships backs your standards push. The HR director who values retention supports your culture initiatives.

Real change happens through coalitions, not solo crusades. These pitfalls of perfectionism, martyrdom and isolation become most visible when theoretical values meet market reality.

Leading Through Values—Viability Crisis: A Personal Lesson

In 2022, I faced a test that would define my approach to values-based leadership. The pharmaceutical company I worked for was the largest private vaccines provider in Sri Lanka, focused on neonatal and paediatric immunisations. While the public health value was clear, the commercial model was breaking because we hadn't revised prices in four years despite rising costs. With Sri Lanka in its worst economic crisis in decades, our margins were collapsing.

Then came the directive from global headquarters: fix the commercial model in ninety days or exit the vaccines portfolio entirely. The contradiction felt impossible. How could we ask for price increases when families were struggling to afford food? Especially when being 'Patient First' was our core value?

But values aren't about avoiding hard choices. They are about finding better solutions.

We assembled a cross-functional team and reframed the challenge, starting not with margins but with a mission: how to maintain vaccine access while ensuring sustainability. Before approaching regulators, we engaged the medical community. We met paediatricians across the country, shared our situation transparently and built support for continued vaccine availability. With their endorsement and a formal letter from the British Embassy backing our presence, we made our case to the authorities.

The result surprised everyone. We secured price increases between 15% and 40% across our portfolio while implementing tiered pricing that protected vulnerable families. We maintained vaccine availability during a national crisis by finding a path that served both values and viability.

That experience taught me that honouring values doesn't mean rejecting commercial reality. It means solving harder problems with greater creativity. Yet individual decisions, no matter how principled, aren't enough. The real challenge? Building systems that support values-based choices when you're not in the room.

Creating the Right Culture for Values-Based Decisions to Thrive

Most organisations put too much faith in individual compliance and too little in designing systems that support it. When pressure hits, people don't rise to values. They fall back on the system around them. Even principled people make poor decisions in broken systems.

Which brings us to the real question: what system are you creating for your people?

Ask yourself:

- Are role expectations clear or is everyone guessing?

- Do incentives reward long-term outcomes or just quarterly wins?
- Can someone raise a red flag without fear of damage to their career?

If your answers are vague, values will be the first thing sacrificed when pressure rises. Your job as a manager is to remove ambiguity by making expectations explicit, aligning incentives to long-term outcomes rather than only quarterly wins and creating the safety for people to raise red flags without risking their careers.

Signalling Leadership Readiness

Senior leaders tracking your performance for elevation watch more than numbers. They're scanning how you lead under pressure. Can you create sustainable advantage without shortcuts? Do your decisions build trust, deepen relationships and withstand market shocks?

These are the real markers of leadership readiness. When ethical dilemmas arise, everything becomes a test. How you frame them. How you communicate your reasoning. How you act when no one's watching. This is your audition for enterprise leadership.

Industries are shifting faster than ever. New business models emerge quarterly. Consumer expectations reset monthly. Roles exist today that didn't five years ago. You'll operate in ambiguous spaces, cutting across functions, geographies and priorities.

Don't resist the messiness. Navigate it. Holding the line on values while proving they drive results marks the true breakthrough. It moves you from running a function to shaping the enterprise. From managing a team to influencing a culture. From executing strategy to defining it.

In unpredictable markets, smart strategy matters. But a leader with a compass matters more.

7

View from the Top with Annaswamy Vaidheesh

To understand what values-driven leadership looks like at the top, I asked Annaswamy Vaidheesh, former managing director of GSK (GlaxoSmithKline) Pharma and Johnson & Johnson India, to share what he looks for when evaluating managers for leadership roles. Vaidheesh gave me my first functional leadership opportunity in 2016 and has spent decades demonstrating how values create sustainable business advantage.[1]

Here's what he had to say.

When I Knew the Call Was Mine

I was running a business unit when internal audit flagged a quality issue with one of our top products. Serious enough to worry about, but not serious enough to mandate a recall. We were three weeks away from quarter-end with real momentum building. Someone suggested a workaround that was technically legal but ethically questionable. I shut down sales until we fixed the problem.

We missed our quarterly target by 10%. Regional leadership wasn't happy. But something shifted after that decision. The team

---

1 See 'Annaswamy Vaidheesh', LinkedIn, https://www.linkedin.com/in/annaswamy-vaidheesh-191082262/.

started trusting me differently. Regulators took note that we had acted before anyone forced us to. Customers heard about it through their networks. That quarter hurt financially, but it bought us genuine credibility that paid dividends for years.

Most companies treat values like wall art. I learnt to weave them into how we actually worked.

In every major decision meeting, someone had to ask whether this aligned with our values. Not as a formality. As a genuine question that could change the outcome. When a potential partner wanted us to bend clinical trial protocols for a ₹50-crore deal, I walked away. Word spread through corridor conversations, not official memos. That's how culture actually shifts: through stories people tell each other at coffee machines.

You won't always get these calls right. I certainly haven't. But when you miss the mark, own it, learn from it and recommit. Your team watches how you handle failures just as closely as your successes.

What I Look for in Promotion Decisions

Three things made a real difference in building integrity across the organisation.

First, we created 'Speak Up' sessions where people could raise ethical concerns face-to-face. The critical element was follow-through. Someone raising an issue in January got a response by March, even if that response explained why we couldn't change something. That reliability built trust.

Second, we celebrated difficult decisions publicly. When our Indonesia team refused to pay facilitation fees and lost market access for six months, we made them heroes at our global meeting. Their experience became part of our organisational identity.

Third, during talent reviews, beyond all the KPIs and metrics, we asked one question: would you trust this person to do the right thing when no one's watching? An immediate yes meant readiness for promotion. Anything less meant they weren't ready, regardless of their numbers.

How I Coach Managers Through Dilemmas

When managers brought ethical dilemmas to my office, I rarely gave direct answers. Instead, I asked: what's really at stake beyond the obvious? What outcome do you fear the most? How this would look in tomorrow's newspaper? Fear drives more poor decisions than greed ever does. The newspaper test, remarkably, clarifies thinking.

One framework consistently helped: examining every decision through three lenses. First, can we legally do this? Second, should we ethically do this? Then, practically, how would we do this? When all three align, you move forward confidently. When they don't, that misalignment tells you something important.

The managers who advance aren't those who hit numbers at any cost. They deliver sustainable results the right way, because values and performance work together when properly understood.

Be willing to ask uncomfortable questions in meetings. Asking 'Are we certain this is the right approach?' becomes career-defining when asked with genuine curiosity rather than judgement.

Start with small steps against casual compromises: inflated expense reports, misleading customer commitments, minor quality shortcuts. These, seemingly, minor moments build your reputation for the bigger decisions ahead.

Most crucially, support your team publicly when they make values-based decisions that cost something tangible. Even when you privately wish they had found a more pragmatic path, that public support develops leaders who will make the right calls when you're not around to guide them.

Values aren't a luxury reserved for good times. They're what carry you through difficult periods.

8
Do-It Notes: Your Values Leadership Road Map

Now it's time to convert values insights into systematic practice. The core question isn't, 'How do I avoid ethical dilemmas?' It's 'How do I architect decisions where principles and performance reinforce each other?' and 'How does integrity become competitive advantage, not a compromise?'

Let's build that system.

Integrity First

'In looking for people to hire, you look for three qualities: integrity, intelligence, and energy. And if they do not have the first, the other two will kill you.'

—*Warren Buffett*

Do-It Notes

This Month: Reveal Your True Operating Values

1. *Audit what actually drives decisions.* Review your last three major wins and three difficult trade-offs. Which principles

really drove those choices? Document the gap between wall posters and closed-door realities.
2. *Interview your team individually.* Ask: 'When pressure hits, what really gets prioritised here?' Then ask: 'What would our competitors say our values are based on our actions?' The answers will sting.
3. *Apply the Five-Question Filter to one live decision.* Choose a current dilemma with real trade-offs. Work through all five questions from Framework 3. Practice now, before pressure intensifies.
4. *Map your vulnerability zones.* Identify three areas where values conflicts are most likely.
   - Regulatory shifts?
   - Social expectations?
   - Technology disruptions?

Pick one. Monitor it thoroughly.

This Quarter: Build Your Values Infrastructure

1. *Create stakeholder sensing loops.* Schedule monthly conversations with three candid advisors. The supplier who knows your competitors. The frontline employee from another function. The customer who'll tell you what you don't want to hear. Ask each one of them: 'What patterns are you noticing?'
2. *Design your values dashboard.* Track three categories that reveal values' health:
   - Reputation: NPS, referral rates, brand sentiment
   - Relationships: retention, renewals, partnership depth
   - Risk: audit findings, compliance trends, near-misses
   - Review monthly. Catch erosion before crisis
3. *Run one values-based experiment.* Pick where ethical clarity might create commercial advantage. Could transparent

pricing differentiate you? Would ethical sourcing open new segments? Pilot it. Measure both trust and revenue.
4. *Lead one cross-functional values initiative.* Whether to choose customer transparency or supplier standards, use it to align multiple teams under one principled banner.

This Year: Scale Values into Competitive Advantage

1. *Embed values into core processes.* Add 'values impact' to every business case template. Include 'how' alongside 'what' in performance reviews. Build integrity criteria into vendor evaluations. Make values systematic, not episodic.
2. *Build your values portfolio.* Document three wins:
   - Crisis prevented (costs avoided)
   - Opportunity unlocked (revenue gained)
   - Relationships strengthened (retention improved)

   Structure these as promotion ammunition.
3. *Develop values reflexes in others.* Guide two high-potentials through three stages. First, they observe your values decisions. Then, they recommend approaches. Finally, they decide with your support. Build the next generation of values leaders.
4. *Craft your signature narrative.* Include 'How Values Drove Performance' in every business review. Show the client won through integrity, the risk avoided by holding standards, the partnership deepened through transparency. Make this your leadership brand.

The Non-Negotiables

Commit to three practices that compound:
- *Weekly*: The values check (thirty minutes). Compare one decision against the stated values. Note the gap.

- *Monthly*: The sensing conversation (one hour). One stakeholder reality check. Listen for uncomfortable truths.
- *Quarterly*: The values audit (two hours). Full review of decisions, gaps and opportunities.

You'll know it's working when:

- Difficult decisions become clearer, not easier.
- Teams raise ethical concerns earlier, not after damage.
- Competitors copy your values-based innovations.
- Customers choose you despite premium pricing.
- Values conflicts shrink while results grow.

Up Next: Trust and Reputation are the Bridge to Enterprise Readiness

You've learnt to lead with a compass. Now we'll put that compass to work across geographies, hierarchies and corporate politics. Many choices will seem to have three right answers, depending on who's asking what.

This is where your reputation differentiates you.

PART 2
NAVIGATION: Advancing Through Complexity

VA**LU**ES

Leveraging Global–Local Dynamics

Global–Local Bridge = Structure + Stakeholders + Sensitivity

In practice: Translate headquarters' strategy for local markets, balance global mandates with on-the-ground realities and build credibility with both audiences.

Unique Reputation

Leadership Brand = Credibility + Visibility + Talent Growth

In practice: Deliver consistently, make your work visible and build a team that reflects your leadership so your influence grows even when you are not in the room.

Section 3: Leveraging Global–Local Dynamics: Translating Global Strategy into Local Wins

At a Glance

Headquarters demands global standardisation. Your local market screams that requirements are different. Your functional head wants efficiency while your country head insists on flexibility. Meanwhile, you're caught in the middle wondering: who actually wins here?

This section helps you navigate that impossible tension. You'll become the bridge rather than choosing sides. You'll turn global–local friction into innovation rather than frustration.

Along the way, you will learn how:

- Picking sides between solid-line and dotted-line bosses nearly derailed my career until I learnt to translate the complexities, not resist;
- Arjun balanced six competing stakeholders and still delivered 15% cost reductions while improving patient outcomes through modular solutions that satisfied everyone;
- Priya achieved 40% higher platform adoption. She navigated between global technology mandates and local banking needs by creating structured dialogue;
- Kavita achieved 35% higher engagement. She bridged global brand consistency with local cultural relevance by translating, not imposing;

You'll master practical frameworks for matrix survival: the Global–Local Integration Framework, Cultural Translation Map and Matrix Navigation Tools to build influence without authority.

To lead across global–local dynamics, you need three things: structure to manage complexity, stakeholder savvy to navigate politics and enough nuance to know when rules need breaking.

9
The Global–Local Tug of War

Your phone buzzes with two back-to-back messages. Your functional head in Singapore asks why the standardised pricing model isn't live yet, demanding consistency across all markets. Your country manager calls: 'Can we talk? You're reporting different Q3 projections to me and to Singapore. Which numbers are real?'

Welcome to the reality of global and matrix organisations, where global ambition meets local truth and you're expected to bridge the two. You're managing not just up but across and diagonally. Multiple bosses, conflicting KPIs and competing definitions of success.

Global companies talk about scale and consistency; local markets demand adaptation. In practice? You're caught between competing priorities from people who all have legitimate claims on your time and targets. The tension runs deeper than geography. Your functional head speaks the language of expertise, standardisation and best practices. Your local head speaks of market dynamics, customer relationships and regulations. Your solid-line boss owns your appraisal. Your dotted-line boss influences your promotion. Both can make or break your career.

Most managers try to pick a side, becoming either the defender of local interests who resists every global initiative or the corporate enforcer who pushes standardisation regardless of market realities.

Both paths lead to the same dead end: limited influence and stalled careers. The ones who survive learn to translate, not take sides.

When Global Directives Met Local Crisis: A Personal Lesson

In 2022, as country GM in Sri Lanka, I faced a test that reshaped how I think about global–local dynamics. Headquarters mandated new packaging standards across all markets. The logic was sound: consistent global branding, streamlined SKUs, standardised sizes. Global teams had spent months designing for efficiency and brand equity. The timeline was aggressive but theoretically achievable.

But Sri Lanka was collapsing economically. Medicine shortages made daily headlines. Import restrictions blocked basic supplies. Inflation hit 60% annually. Fuel queues stretched for kilometres. My team worked around the clock just keeping essential drugs in stock.

When I presented our reality to global leadership, they responded firmly: 'Every market has challenges. We can't make exceptions.' My local team's disbelief was palpable when I told them we needed to prioritise packaging changes. 'Have you lost touch with what's happening here?' they asked.

I found myself defending positions I didn't believe, arguing for flexibility to global teams that sounded like resistance while pushing mandates to local teams that seemed absurd given the crisis.

My supply chain director, a veteran of crisis markets, reframed the problem entirely. 'You're treating this as a battle between global and local. What if it's a translation problem instead?'

We changed our approach completely. Rather than explaining why directives wouldn't work, we brought headquarters into our reality. Virtual sessions showed pharmacists managing empty shelves. Hospital administrators describing patients having to share medications due to supply shortages. Distributors explaining the daily challenge of finding fuel.

The Global–Local Tug of War 71

Once the global team understood the context, the conversation shifted. Headquarters kept the standards but slowed the rollout to protect supply. Together, we designed a solution serving both needs. Essential medicines retained existing packaging for six months to avoid disruption, while non-critical products transitioned immediately, demonstrating commitment to global standards.

The global team later adopted our 'crisis protocol' for other volatile markets. What began as resistance became a model that others copied. That experience revealed something fundamental about navigating organisational tensions. When you stop defending sides and start translating context, you become the bridge.

The most successful matrix leaders don't identify as being global or local, functional or regional. They're integrators who make complex organisational designs deliver results. They understand that global strategies succeed through local execution. Local ideas only matter if global systems can carry them.

Priya, Arjun and Kavita each discovered this truth in their own way.

Priya's Challenge: When Global Platforms Meet Local Realities

'This platform will transform banking across South Asia,' the London tech director announced on the video call, promising a 35% cost reduction and eighteen-month rollout since it was already live in Europe.

Priya watched her country managers' faces on-screen, reading scepticism mixed with the resignation of people who had heard these promises before. As head of institutional banking strategy, Priya had to deploy the platform across India, Bangladesh and Sri Lanka—three radically different markets with distinct banking ecosystems.

The platform was built for European realities: high digital literacy, harmonised regulations, reliable infrastructure. South Asia operated differently. Indian customers had leapfrogged traditional banking for mobile wallets. Bangladesh still valued personal relationships alongside technology. Sri Lanka's data localisation rules made European compliance look simple.

Three markets, three completely different games.

The disconnect became clear during monthly calls, as London measured deployment speed and cost savings, while country managers tracked customer satisfaction and the compliance team tallied potential violations. Each group spoke a different language, measured different things and solved different problems.

'This platform works,' the global director insisted during one tense call. 'Local requirements are just implementation details.'

Priya watched the same conversation being repeated month after month, with everyone defending their corner while the gap between global vision and local reality widened. She chose to build bridges instead of defending positions. She launched global–local alignment sessions rather than proposing another compromise. Technology leaders in London sat virtually with operations teams in Dhaka, Colombo and Mumbai. For the first time, headquarters saw ground-level challenges, while local teams understood technical constraints.

These sessions revealed what emails never could. Regulatory requirements weren't roadblocks but competitive advantages when properly integrated. Many local needs could be met through configuration, not customisation. The gap wasn't as wide as it seemed. Everyone had been solving for the wrong problem.

Together, they designed a three-layer architecture:

- *Core platform*: 70% standardisation for security and efficiency

The Global–Local Tug of War

- *Regional layer:* 20% South Asian features, like payment integrations and language support
- *Local layer:* 10% for country-specific compliance and customer journeys

Modularity became the bridge between global and local.

The rollout took six months longer than London planned, but the results justified the delay. Customer adoption exceeded European benchmarks by 40%, and cost savings surpassed projections once the platform no longer required constant fixes. The model became the blueprint for all emerging market deployments.

Pause and Reflect

Influence multiplies when stakeholders persuade each other, not when you persuade them one by one.

- Who are the stakeholders you influence but don't control?
- Do you mediate between opposing views or create spaces where those views evolve together?

Sometimes the issue isn't navigating politics but solving problems where every solution seems to require choosing winners and losers.

Arjun's Matrix Challenge: The Universal Formulation Dilemma

When Arjun read the email from headquarters, he sat staring at the screen. Effective immediately, all diabetes formulations would follow the new global standard without exceptions. Two years of localisation work, scrapped.

As the head of product development for India and Southeast Asia, Arjun navigated a complex web of relationships. Global

R&D controlled his budget and wanted standardisation. Regional commercial teams set his targets and pushed for market growth. Country managers across multiple markets determined his success through their local results.

The global logic seemed compelling. One formulation meant streamlined manufacturing, simplified regulatory filings and massive cost savings. But Arjun knew what those spreadsheets missed. India's formulations handled tropical storage and rural patients who split medications among families. Thailand's colour-coded packaging helped patients with limited literacy manage dosing. The Philippines had tiered formulations for government programmes. Every market had solved real problems the global standard ignored.

On a tense video call spanning three time zones, positions hardened. 'We need to think beyond individual markets,' his global director insisted. 'Local preferences can't dictate global strategy.'

Thailand's country manager pushed back: 'That's fine for headquarters, but it doesn't help the diabetic grandmother who can't read dosing instructions. We'll lose patients.'

India's head added, 'Our tropical formulation prevents degradation in extreme heat without refrigeration. The global standard assumes cold chain distribution we don't have.'

Each group had different metrics and pressures with little interest in compromise.

That weekend, instead of drafting another defensive email, Arjun sketched a different possibility. What if standardisation and localisation weren't opposites? What if they could work together? The answer was hidden in the question.

After a week of calculations, he developed modular standardisation:

- *Core platform*: 70% standardised active ingredients and base formulation, delivering the cost savings the global team wanted;

The Global–Local Tug of War   75

- *Local flexibility*: 30% for packaging, dosing mechanisms and patient education, ensuring medicines actually got taken.

Both-and instead of either-or.

When he presented this to global leadership, his director was sceptical, saying this wasn't the standardisation they had requested.

'It's better,' Arjun replied. 'You get 70% cost savings and simplified regulation. Markets keep the 30% that determine whether patients actually take the medicine. Without adherence, the best formulation is worthless.'

The proposal faced immediate pushback as the global team worried about losing control, regional teams questioned the complexity and country teams wondered if 30% flexibility was enough.

Instead of endless debate, Arjun launched pilots in India and Thailand where stakes were highest. He knew data would persuade better than arguments.

Six months later, the data spoke. Manufacturing costs dropped 15% through standardisation. Patient adherence improved 12% through local adaptations. The company adopted Arjun's model as the new standard. What had started as resistance became the blueprint for all therapeutic areas. Arjun's real innovation wasn't the modular design but reframing the conversation.

In matrix organisations, success doesn't come from choosing between competing demands. It comes from redesigning systems to satisfy multiple stakeholders simultaneously.

Stop picking sides. Start building bridges.

Pause and Reflect

The best solutions let both sides claim victory instead of forcing a choice between them. Real innovation lives in the space between competing demands. It's where 'either-or' becomes 'both-and'. Where creative tension produces breakthrough thinking.

Ask yourself:

- Where are you stuck between competing demands that seem irreconcilable?
- What would a solution look like if both stakeholders could claim victory?

Sometimes stakeholder alignment fails not because of conflicting interests but because of cultural misunderstanding.

Kavita's Challenge: When Global Messages Get Lost in Translation

The campaign video ended in silence in the conference room, before the creative director from New York announced that it had tested off the charts in the US and Europe for its message of self-empowerment, personal achievement and universal appeal.

Kavita watched it again later on her laptop. A young woman backpacking solo through Europe, choosing adventure over family obligations. Stunning production values. A message built for New York or London. She knew it would fall flat in her markets.

As regional marketing director for beauty in India and Southeast Asia, Kavita faced an immediate crisis. Global wanted the campaign live across her markets in twelve weeks: same visuals, same message, same everything. They had spent millions and were convinced they had cracked the code for reaching millennial women worldwide.

The disconnect was stark. In her markets, solo female travel raised concerns about safety and family harmony, not aspirations for freedom. A Mumbai focus group confirmed her fears. One participant asked if the woman had been abandoned. Another called it foreign. Several looked actively uncomfortable. This campaign would die in Asia.

The organisational complexity hit hard. New York controlled budget and brand guidelines, demanding zero deviation. Regional sales needed materials that would actually sell products. Local teams knew the campaign would fail but felt powerless against the global mandate.

The planning call quickly turned tense. 'Brand consistency is non-negotiable,' the global director said. 'We can't have different stories in different markets.'

The Indonesia manager pushed back: 'Then prepare for failure. This message actively alienates our customers.'

Kavita shifted the conversation. 'What if we're not changing the story, but translating it?'

She proposed keeping the core emotion of self-empowerment but expressing it through regional values. In India, a young woman starting her business with family support. In Indonesia, friends achieving dreams together. In Vietnam, individual growth benefiting the community. 'Same brand promise, different cultural expression,' she said.

The turning point came when the global creative director watched a Jakarta focus group. Participants who were cold to the original campaign lit up at the localised version. Same colours, music and emotional arc; this time it showed friends supporting one another. The energy shift was obvious.

Kavita developed a precise framework:

- Non-negotiables: brand colours, logo placement, music, emotional arc
- Adaptable: narrative structure, casting, cultural contexts

Same feeling, different expression.

Managing consistency across markets proved brutal: each country pushed boundaries while the global team pulled back. Kavita assembled mixed teams of local experts and global brand guardians, ensuring messages stayed true yet resonated locally.

The results silenced all sceptics. Visual alignment hit 85% across markets: consistent enough for global, distinct enough for local. Engagement jumped 35% above previous campaigns. The framework became mandatory for all global campaigns.

The regional president called it 'the difference between being global and being globally relevant'.

Pause and Reflect

Cultural differences are translation challenges, not resistance. Adaptation strengthens your message by ensuring it can be heard.

- When global and local clash, do you pick sides or build bridges?
- Can you help both stakeholders see their success in a shared solution?

Up Next: The Frameworks to Manage Global–Local Dynamics

If you're caught between functional agendas and regional tensions, unsure whether to escalate or align, you're not alone. Most managers learn matrix navigation the hard way. It's rarely taught in formal training. You discover it through painful trial and error.

In the next chapter, you'll learn frameworks to stop being the messenger and start being the integrator—someone who connects global ambition with local intelligence.

10

The Both-And Solution

Most managers get trapped between global mandates and local realities, defending one against the other. Those who advance to leadership understand something different. Global–local tension isn't a problem to solve, but a polarity to leverage. They find shared wins across competing scorecards, translate strategy without losing local intelligence and influence without formal authority.

They master the both-and solution.

> **Frameworks in this chapter**
>
> **70-20-10 Architecture**
> Purpose: Define what is fixed, what flexes and what is custom.
>
> **Shared-Wins Scorecard**
> Purpose: Tie teams to one golden thread of metrics across levels.
>
> **The Dubbing Strategy**
> Purpose: Keep the same story while adapting voice, examples and proof locally.

Framework 1: 70-20-10 Architecture (Global core, regional flex, local custom)

Stop choosing between global and local. Start designing systems that leverage both. Standardise what drives efficiency. Adapt what drives effectiveness. This is how you turn tension into advantage:

Step 1: Decode What's Really at Stake

When global directives clash with local realities, resist defending or complying. Decode the underlying needs instead.

Global wants: Cost efficiency through scale. Risk mitigation through proven approaches. Simplified governance. Brand coherence.

Local needs: Market responsiveness. Cultural alignment. Operational feasibility. Regulatory compliance.

Document these as design requirements, not competing demands. The breakthrough comes when you see how they reinforce rather than contradict each other.

Step 2: Design Your Three-Layer Architecture

Build solutions with three connected layers:

- *Global core (60–70%)*: The foundation that never changes: safety protocols, financial standards, technology architecture, core brand elements. This drives scale and ensures compliance.
- *Regional adaptation (20–30%)*: The flexible middle: go-to-market approaches, pricing structures, distribution models, communication styles. This balances efficiency with relevance.

- *Local customisation (10–20%)*: The market-specific outer layer: cultural expressions, payment methods, service approaches, last-mile solutions. This ensures genuine effectiveness.

Think of it as a wedding cake: same base, regional flavours, local decoration.

Step 3: Build Integration Mechanisms

Layers without connectors create chaos.

Decision rights: Who decides what goes where? When can local needs override global wants? How do regions escalate? Clarity here prevents every decision from becoming a negotiation.

Feedback loops: Local innovations strengthen global standards. Global capabilities enhance local execution. Innovation emerges anywhere; capture it systematically.

Balanced metrics: Measure both global consistency and local performance. One-sided metrics drive dysfunction.

Making It Work: Start with one global–local conflict you're facing now. Map it using the three-layer model. Design a pilot with roughly 70% global standardisation and 30% local adaptation. Measure results on both scorecards.

These percentages are starting points. Regulated industries might need 80% standardisation. Diverse consumer markets might need 40% local adaptation. What matters is deliberate design, not ad hoc compromises.

Framework 2: Shared-Wins Scorecard (Tie everyone to one thread of metrics)

In global organisations, every stakeholder optimises for different metrics. This isn't dysfunction, it's intentional design. The key is turning competing scorecards into complementary forces. Stop trying to align everyone. Start finding where different goals intersect.

Step 1: Map the Real Scorecards

Forget official KPIs. Look at what really drives decisions:
Global functional heads want: Standardisation metrics. Board narratives. Budget predictability. Cross-market efficiency.
Regional leaders juggle: Growth targets. Portfolio performance. Talent retention. Regional influence.
Country managers need: Local P&L performance. Government relations. Team morale. Market opportunities.
When you understand these real drivers, you will find common ground.

Step 2: Identify the Golden Threads

Look for metrics that appear everywhere, just labelled differently. The key is finding the functional equivalent.
Customer satisfaction becomes: NPS for marketing. Retention for sales. Ticket volume for service. Reputation for country managers.
Operational efficiency becomes: Cost per unit for finance. Productivity for operations. Resource allocation for regional heads. Speed to market for product teams.
These convergence points transform competition into collaboration.

Step 3: Architect Multi-Win Solutions

Structure every proposal with this formula:

1. Frame the shared challenge everyone recognises

2. Show specific wins for each stakeholder's priorities
3. Quantify the collective benefit no one can achieve alone

Example in action: 'Our modular platform reduces global tech costs by 30% (functional win), enables local features in days, not months (country win) and improves customer satisfaction everywhere (shared win).'

Make wins concrete and measurable. 'Better alignment' moves no one.

Making It Work: Pick three critical stakeholders for your current initiative. Map what really drives their decisions. Find two metrics they all care about, even if they all label it differently. Design your next proposal to show explicit wins on all three scorecards.

Don't make everyone want the same thing. Show how your proposal helps each get more of what they already want. This shift from persuasion to translation makes you invaluable.

Framework 3: The Dubbing Strategy (Same story, different voices, one message)

Global strategies often fail not because they're wrong, but because they're lost in translation.

Different cultures process information through different lenses. Same message, different delivery. The goal is reaching diverse audiences without changing your core message.

Master translation, master influence.

Step 1: Map Cultural Operating Systems

Before you communicate an initiative, understand how each group prefers to decide and absorb information.

Decision styles: Hierarchical cultures defer to seniority, consensus cultures seek harmony, individualist cultures value speed and analytic cultures ask for evidence before endorsement.

Information sequence: Some audiences want the full context first and the recommendation later, while others expect the conclusion upfront and the logic after. Many groups want trust and intent established before content; some insist on proof before persuasion.

Risk orientation: Risk-averse teams want detailed mitigations and clear stop points, risk-tolerant teams welcome experiments and risk-aware teams expect contingencies and ranges.

A presentation that succeeds in New York may struggle in Tokyo, not because the content is flawed, but because the delivery did not match local expectations about deference, sequence and acceptable risk.

Step 2: Design Your Translation Architecture

Effective translation works across three layers. Think of it as dubbing a film so it plays well in every market while the story remains intact.

Universal core: (Does not change.) State the value proposition, the measurable outcomes, the quality or compliance standards, and the strategic intent. This is the script you will not alter.

Cultural adaptation: (Flexes by audience.) Adjust the order of information, the types of evidence you foreground, the pace of rollout, and the communication channels. For example, lead with benchmark data for an analytic audience, or lead with sponsor intent and team impact for a relationship-oriented audience.

Local expression: (Fully customised.) Use local examples, familiar metaphors, trusted messengers and accepted professional norms. This could mean a respected country leader presenting the deck, a short briefing in the local language or a town hall that allows questions before formal sign-off.

Step 3: Build Translation Bridges

Find translators: Identify insiders who understand both the global intent and the local culture and can explain each side to the other. Give them early drafts and authority to propose changes in order, tone and proof.

Test and refine: Pilot with a small group first, capture what lands and what confuses and update the deck and talking points accordingly.

Create templates: For common initiatives, provide a simple template that shows what is fixed and what is flexible so teams do not reinvent the wheel.

Measure effectiveness: Low adoption often signals a translation problem rather than a strategy problem. Track first-week questions, opt-in rates and time to first milestone to see where the message is failing to travel.

Translation in practice: Consider a global efficiency drive that seeks a 20% cost reduction to fund innovation. Begin with one market, learn what motivates action and expand from there. Lead with benchmarks and return on investment for efficiency-focused cultures, highlight job protection and team growth for relationship-focused cultures and frame savings as fuel for future products in innovation-driven cultures. The destination is the same, while the path changes with what each audience needs to hear first in order to move.

The 70:20:10 Mindset

In global–local work, influence behaves like capital. You cannot spend it everywhere, so you allocate it. My rule of thumb is a 70:20:10 split that keeps you effective without being expended on battles that do not matter.

The first 70% goes to adaptation. Take the global objective and make it work locally. This is not surrender. It is disciplined flexibility. You align on intent, translate the how and remove local friction so the plan lands in the market you know best.

The next 20% goes to mutual adjustment. Use this to reshape the plan where local insight improves the outcome. Pick your moments, bring evidence and push for changes that raise the probability of success for everyone. The goal is not to win an argument. The goal is to make the global plan smarter.

The final 10% is letting go. Some mandates will fail on their own. Some wins cost more than they return. Choose not to spend political capital when the business can afford a learning cycle or when the relationship matters more than being right.

Treat this as portfolio management. Most of your influence funds proven strategies that need tuning. Some of it backs high-leverage changes where your market knowledge is unique. A small reserve is held back so you can walk away from low-yield fights. That is how you stay useful in a matrix. You are not just surviving the tension between headquarters and market. You are directing it towards results.

Here is a personal story of what happens when you mistake visibility for alignment.

Who's the Real Boss? A Personal Lesson in Power and Perception

In 2017, I was general manager for sales and marketing excellence at the India affiliate of a global pharmaceutical company. Like many matrix roles, it came with two bosses and one constant balancing act. I had a solid line to the VP of commercial excellence in India, my functional manager, and a dotted line to the regional director in Istanbul, who controlled visibility, cross-country projects and pathways to regional roles.

On paper it was manageable. In practice it was a tightrope. The regional director had a magnetic presence. He was charismatic, politically savvy and always ahead of the conversation, so I gravitated towards him. His projects felt bigger, and his circle was more influential. I began prioritising his requests, adopting his language and aligning with his vision. At times I forgot to inform my local manager; at other times I chose not to, caught up in the momentum of regional initiatives.

The balance was delicate, and I misjudged it. At first it felt strategic: build global capital, stay close to power. Then the cracks appeared. My local boss heard about initiatives from others. He learnt about projects after they started, or not at all.

I'd become invisible to the person who actually controlled my career.

During year-end feedback, reality hit when he looked at me calmly and said, 'Sunder, you are based in Mumbai, but your focus seems to be Istanbul. Your payroll still gets processed here.' It stung because it was true, delivered without sarcasm but with disappointment.

In chasing regional visibility, I had neglected local alignment and confused proximity to power with actual influence. My appraisal reflected this with a credibility hit that lasted longer than the rating.

The lesson was clear. Dotted lines open doors. Solid lines build foundations. Global visibility matters, but local credibility enables it. Chase one without the other and you'll have neither.

Now, when I see coaching managers caught between reporting lines, I share this story. The job is not to choose between local and global, but to be the translator who helps both succeed. Chase visibility without alignment, and you will find yourself trusted by neither side. Success comes not from picking sides but from bridging them effectively.

Signalling Leadership Readiness

Senior leaders recognise global–local navigation capability through specific signals.

You build coalitions without formal authority. You design solutions where multiple stakeholders claim victory. You translate fluently across perspectives representing local realities in global forums while helping local teams understand global logic.

You turn structural tensions into innovation opportunities. Most tellingly, you become the person others call when global and local interests collide. Not because you have authority to resolve conflicts. Not because you control resources. But because you have the capability to find integration where others see only conflict.

This reputation for handling complexity becomes your career currency. The path from middle management to leadership isn't about years of experience or team size. It's about demonstrating three things. You see systems, not pieces. You create value across boundaries, not just within them. You turn organisational complexity from burden into advantage.

Master global–local navigation, and you signal readiness for leadership roles.

11
View from the Top with Hariram Krishnan

To understand what it takes to lead across global–local boundaries, I asked Hariram Krishnan, former managing director of Galderma India and executive coach to CEOs, to share what he looks for when evaluating managers for broader roles. Hari Sir, as I call him, was my first coach when I moved to a global pharmaceutical firm in 2014.[1] *Here's what he had to say.*

Finding the Bridge Between Global and Local

Leading across global–local boundaries isn't about choosing sides. It's about creating connections that honour both global strategy and local truth.

We were handling a global product with strong brand equity worldwide but a completely different reality in India. The product was imported and priced at a premium, putting it out of reach for most patients who desperately needed it. Global headquarters wanted to protect the premium positioning. They feared local manufacturing would dilute brand value and invite generic competition.

---

1   See 'Hariram Krishnan', LinkedIn, https://www.linkedin.com/in/hariram-krishnan-26a6a57/.

I could see the local truth clearly. Without addressing affordability, we'd have a prestigious product that helped no one. The goal was to find a bridge between these seemingly incompatible realities.

We built our case carefully, using patient stories and physician observations to show how local manufacturing could expand access without compromising quality. We framed it not as breaking global strategy but as extending its impact. We demonstrated how we could reach more patients, build stronger market presence and still protect technology through carefully structured IP agreements.

The execution required tremendous patience. We worked methodically through regulatory approvals, ensured our quality benchmarks exactly matched global standards and gradually shifted to local production. The result exceeded everyone's expectations. We tripled patient access while maintaining premium positioning in our segment.

What I learnt stays with me today. The global–local balance isn't about compromise or choosing the middle ground. It's about finding where global intent meets local reality. Quality, consistency and brand value meeting access, affordability and cultural relevance—that intersection is where real impact happens.

What I Look for: Trust in Matrix Structures

In matrix structures where authority is distributed across multiple reporting lines, trust becomes your real currency. Building trust meant demonstrating three things consistently: credibility through genuine expertise, reliability by keeping every commitment and genuinely listening to understand different perspectives rather than waiting for my turn to speak.

I once coordinated a product launch across functions that didn't report to me: supply chain, marketing and medical affairs. The project was already behind schedule when I inherited it. Each function blamed the others for the delays. Authority wouldn't have helped in this situation, but transparency did.

I created a simple dashboard showing how each delay cascaded through the entire system. Regulatory slipping by a week meant marketing could immediately see the impact on their media buys and adjust accordingly.

The real breakthrough came through translation between functions. Marketing spoke in terms of reach and impressions. Medical talked about efficacy and adverse events. Supply chain focused on batch sizes and lead times. My job became helping each function understand how their decisions impacted others across the organisation. Once that understanding emerged naturally, trust followed. Alignment became automatic rather than forced.

Cultural Navigation Without Cultural Mastery

Early in my career, I made predictable mistakes. I pushed for quick decisions in Asian meetings and received only silence. I invested heavily in relationship-building during European meetings and got feedback that I was wasting valuable time. After two failures, I learnt one crucial lesson: listen twice before acting once.

Instead of trying to master every cultural nuance, I developed practices that travelled well across all cultures. For Asian teams, I scheduled pre-meetings where they could align among themselves before the main discussion. For European teams, I sent detailed pre-reads so we could dive straight into decisions without lengthy context-setting. For American teams, I kept meetings short but scheduled them frequently to maintain momentum.

Effective cross-border leadership isn't about knowing every culture perfectly. It's about building shared rituals of respect and clarity that work regardless of geography, while remaining authentic to your own leadership style.

The managers I've watched succeed in global–local roles share one quality: they treat cultural differences as translation challenges, not obstacles. They don't try to be everything to everyone. They find ways to honour both global consistency and local relevance, creating value neither side could achieve alone.

12
Do-It Notes: Your Global–Local Navigation Road Map

Now it's time to convert global–local insights into systematic practice. The core question isn't 'How do I manage matrix politics?'. It's 'How do I architect solutions that align competing stakeholders?'. Not through compromise or capitulation, but through strategic integration.

Check for Clarity

'The single biggest problem in communication is the illusion that it has taken place.'

—*George Bernard Shaw*

Do-It Notes

This Month: Map Your Matrix Reality

1. *Audit your current tensions.* List three major global–local conflicts from the past quarter. What was really at stake beyond surface disagreements? Which of these were

resolved through compromise versus integration? The patterns will surprise you.
2. *Decode stakeholder priorities.* Interview three people from different parts of your matrix. The global pusher of standardisation. The local resister of mandates. The regional person caught between. Ask each one: 'When global and local clash, which of the two usually wins?'
3. *Apply the Three-Layer Framework.* Take one global mandate that feels locally unsuitable. Map what must stay global (60–70%), what can be adapted regionally (20–30%) and what needs local customisation (10–20%). Present this redesign to your team and capture their objections and proposed changes. Convert the feedback into a one-page addendum that lists must-haves versus nice-to-haves, updates the percentages where the evidence is strong, names decision owners for each layer and defines service levels for handoffs. Pilot the revised design on one market or process for thirty days with two success metrics that both global and local accept, and agree on an escalation path if a threshold is missed.
4. *Find golden threads.* Identify two metrics that both global and local care about, even if they label them differently. Customer satisfaction might be NPS for one, retention for another. These become your integration points.

This Quarter: Build Your Bridge Systems

1. *Create stakeholder convergence maps.* Meet separately with someone global and someone local. Ask each of them: 'What does success look like for you?' Document where their definitions overlap. That's your opportunity space.
2. *Run one integration experiment.* Pick where global–local conflict costs money or time. Could modular design

reduce conflict? Could cultural translation improve adoption? Design a pilot serving both priorities. Measure both scorecards.

    Build translation templates. Create three versions of one initiative for different cultural contexts. Test with small groups. Document what needed adaptation versus what stayed constant. This becomes your playbook.

3. *Lead one cross-boundary initiative.* Own a task that requires matrix navigation, such as implementing a global platform locally or scaling local innovation globally.

This Year: Become the Integration Architect

1. *Embed integration into processes.* Add 'global–local impact' fields to every proposal template. Include cross-boundary metrics in performance reviews. For every decision, ask, 'Who else needs to win?' Make integration thinking automatic.
2. *Build your integration portfolio.* Document three wins:
   - Global–local conflict turned into innovation
   - Both efficiency and effectiveness achieved
   - Coalition built across competing stakeholders

   Structure these as promotion case studies.
3. *Develop matrix navigators.* Pick two high-potential managers, one direct report and one cross-functional peer at a key handoff. Week 1, they shadow your stakeholder meetings and debrief for ten minutes on decision rights and trade-offs. Week 2, they translate a global memo for your market and present it to you and a local lead. Week 3, they run one integration meeting to align global requirements, regional pacing and local execution, and you give same-day notes.

4. *Craft your signature narrative.* In business reviews, include consistent examples of bridging global and local initiatives: the system implementation that preserved local innovation; the cost initiative that improved both efficiency and responsiveness; the cultural translation that made global strategy locally successful. Make integration your leadership brand.
5. *Track your navigation dashboard.* Monitor three indicators:
    - Integration wins (both global and local successful)
    - Translation effectiveness (adoption rates across cultures)
    - Network strength (cross-boundary relationships activated)

The Non-Negotiables: Commit to three practices that build global–local mastery.
- *Weekly*: The stakeholder check-in (thirty minutes). One conversation with someone from a different part of the matrix to learn their reality.
- *Monthly*: The integration audit (thirty minutes). Review one decision for global–local impact. What worked? What didn't?
- *Quarterly*: The translation test (two hours). Adapt one message for three different audiences. Test what resonates.

These compound over time into unconscious competence.

You'll know it's working when:

- Global stops seeing you as an obstructionist
- Local stops seeing you as an enforcer
- Both start seeing you as an enabler

Do-It Notes: Your Global–Local Navigation Road Map

- Conflicts decrease while innovation increases
- You're invited to broker other people's challenges

The ultimate signal? When your phone rings first during global–local crises.

Up Next

You've mastered the matrix. You've become the translator. You've turned tension into innovation. Now it's time to make that capability visible. To build a reputation that opens doors before you knock.

Welcome to the politics of perception.

Section 4: Unique Reputation: Making Yourself Visible and in Demand

At a Glance

Senior leaders entrust certain managers with their most critical initiatives. High performers choose specific teams to stay on. Few managers become known for something distinctive. In an organisation full of capable peers, what makes you memorable?

This section shows how to build a leadership reputation that opens doors, attracts talent and accelerates your career through consistent, visible impact rather than self-promotion.

Along the way, you will learn how:

- I discovered an uncomfortable truth about reputation during my first months as country GM. Everything I thought about proving myself was counterproductive.
- Arjun turned public failure into signature strength. He created a culture of transparent learning that became his leadership brand.
- Priya moved from being an invisible player to a visible strategist. She owned her narrative, presented her own work and built external validation.
- Kavita escaped being pigeonholed as 'just a brand expert'. She deliberately took on supply chain optimisation, proved her range and earned the regional role.
- You can master practical frameworks for reputation building. The Visibility Strategy Model, Range Expansion Method and systematic approaches to establish leadership identity.

To build a strong leadership brand, you need to deliver consistently, be seen for the right reasons, and grow others who thrive because of you.

13

When Reputation Becomes Reality

You've just been promoted to regional director and inherited a team that's been without stable leadership for six months. As you settle into the role, three discoveries reveal the leadership reputation you've inherited from your predecessor.

During your first team meeting, you ask for innovative ideas to improve productivity. Silence. Then one brave soul suggests 'better documentation' before quickly adding, 'if that's OK with you'. You realise the previous leader's 'collaborative approach' had trained the team to wait for permission rather than take initiative.

Your one-on-ones reveal another pattern. Each person brings a list of minor decisions awaiting your approval, from vendor selections to meeting schedules. Your predecessor's 'attention to detail' became micromanagement that stripped away their confidence and agency. They were taught to comply, not contribute.

The most telling moment comes when the regional VP pulls you aside after a leadership meeting and says, 'I'm hoping you can rebuild trust with that team because they've become invisible to the rest of the organisation, and we need their expertise front and centre.'

These three moments show something crucial: your predecessor's leadership didn't leave with them; it lingered in every hesitant decision, every request for approval and every missed opportunity for the team to shine.

This inherited damage is one thing, but sometimes you create it when the need to prove yourself becomes the very thing that diminishes your team.

When Proving Yourself Proves Counterproductive: A Personal Lesson

The country GM role I had secured after years in functional leadership brought immediate challenges. I took over a team of hundred people who felt overlooked by regional leadership, convinced their work didn't matter despite consistent effort. This invisibility was evident everywhere. Hesitation to share wins. Achievements buried in reports. No Sri Lankan names on high-potential lists. The team internalised their irrelevance so deeply they had stopped trying to be seen.

Fresh in the role and eager to justify my appointment, I spent three months demonstrating expertise at every opportunity. When the team presented challenges, I offered solutions from past experience. When they shared local insights, I imposed global frameworks. When they struggled, I showed them 'better' ways.

But in reality, the impact of my actions was quite the opposite. Nirupa Wijeratne, my HR director, revealed the truth with one observation: 'The team feels like you don't trust them to do their jobs.'

That feedback forced an uncomfortable examination. By jumping in with solutions, I prevented them from developing problem-solving capabilities. By imposing frameworks, I dismissed local expertise. By showing 'better' ways, I reinforced their belief they weren't good enough. In trying to prove I could lead them to visibility, I was making them more invisible.

The transformation began when I shifted from demonstrating my capability to showcasing theirs. Instead of solving problems, I had them present solutions to regional leadership. Rather than translating their work, I helped the global team understand local context. When opportunities arose, I became an advocate, not an expert.

Within six months, two team members joined regional committees, our insights shaped strategy and Sri Lanka was recognised as an innovation hub. When economic collapse hit later, regional leadership sought our guidance on managing volatility. We had established a reputation for expertise and not just execution.

The lasting lesson forced me to confront uncomfortable questions. Did people become more confident or more cautious when I entered a room? Did I create space for others' expertise or fill it with my own? Did my team become more visible or only my leadership? The answers hurt.

Building your reputation directly often diminishes it, while building others' reputations establishes yours more powerfully than self-promotion ever could. Leadership reputation isn't what you project but what you enable in others.

Arjun, Priya and Kavita each discovered this truth through defining moments that transformed not only their approach to leadership but also how others experienced it.

Arjun's Reputation Test: When Failure Defines You or Refines You

Arjun had spent five years building his reputation as the executive who always delivered. Senior leadership called him 'the safe pair of hands', trusting him with their most sensitive projects.

That reputation crumbled when his division's flagship project failed after two years and eroded millions in investment. The failure threatened three other initiatives, sending teams into crisis mode.

Advice poured in immediately. His mentor cautioned: 'Leadership wants someone to blame, not martyrs.' A peer suggested: 'You've only run this division for six months. These were inherited problems.' The regional president was blunt: 'Everyone knows who pushed this approach. Make that clear.'

Each suggestion made political sense because other leaders often navigated failure by finding scapegoats or deflecting, but Arjun had built his career on ownership and protecting his teams. Simply absorbing blame would destroy his credibility without fixing what caused the failure.

So Arjun chose differently. When presenting to global leadership, he didn't blame individuals but exposed systemic failures. He showed how their culture rewarded confirming biases over raising concerns, and how risk reviews checked boxes rather than question assumptions. 'This isn't about who made wrong choices,' he told the executives. 'It's about why our system let those choices go unchallenged for two years.'

The room went quiet. Some worried the transparency would damage the division. A few peers called him naïve. But Arjun pressed forward. He had nothing left to lose and everything to build.

He introduced 'Failure Fridays', where teams analysed mistakes without fear. He shared failure analyses across divisions in the spirit that expensive mistakes should at least help others learn. He brought external experts to audit processes and published findings internally.

Transparency became his weapon against dysfunction.

Results came within six months with late-stage failures dropping 40% and hidden problems surfacing in weeks instead of months. Talented people requested transfers to his division, drawn to an environment that treated mistakes as learning opportunities.

At the annual summit, the CEO recognised Arjun's transformation: 'Some leaders let failure define them. Others use it to transform organisations. Arjun showed us the second path.'

By choosing transparency over self-protection, Arjun evolved from a 'safe pair of hands' to a catalyst for organisational learning.

Pause and Reflect

How you respond to visible failure shapes reputation more powerfully than a dozen quiet successes. When failure becomes public, you face a choice. Protect yourself or fix the system. Manage perception or address reality.

- When facing reputation-defining crisis, do you protect yourself or address root causes?
- Does your response to failure strengthen the organisation or just your image?

Sometimes the problem isn't recovering from failure but being excellent yet invisible.

Priya's Strategic Pivot: From Invisible Architect to Visible Strategist

Priya had engineered the bank's most successful customer acquisition strategy, driving consistent growth through her segmentation models and analytics frameworks. Yet when she watched the quarterly leadership review, she was mentioned only as 'solid analytical support'.

As commercial banking strategy lead for South Asia, Priya had fallen into a limiting pattern: she built engines that drove success but let others drive them publicly. Her segmentation model was suddenly being credited to the Malaysia head. Her approach became the regional team's strategy. Her analytics engine became everyone's achievement except hers.

The comfortable narrative would be to blame others for taking credit. But Priya's mentor asked a harder question: 'If you're not telling your own story, why are you surprised when others write you out of it?'

That forced an uncomfortable examination. She had believed excellent work spoke for itself. That sending analyses to country heads was enough. That being the enabler mattered more than being the spokesperson. This belief system made her crucial but invisible.

Priya's transformation was about visible ownership tied to revenue. She replaced fifty-slide packs with a five-slide brief that covered the problem, the segmentation thesis, test results, commercial impact and the decision she wanted. She stopped emailing decks and began presenting in quarterly reviews, opening with the two metrics her model moved and closing with the approval request. She named the method 'Segment Lift 3x', issued a one-page decision memo that captured attribution and go-live and asked partner teams to credit the originating model on slide one. She also ran a monthly forty-minute 'analysis to action' session for sales, walking through one win and the choices that made it work.

The breakthrough came when she realised internal visibility had limits without external validation. She began speaking at banking forums and sharing insights on LinkedIn. Her posts sparked discussions beyond her immediate network, and senior leaders who had never noticed her internally began engaging with her work. Within a year, she was promoted to regional head of strategic initiatives and recognised as a strategist, not an analyst.

Priya stopped waiting for recognition and started ensuring it couldn't be missed. The shift changed not only how others saw her but how she saw her role in shaping reputation.

Pause and Reflect

Great work builds your reputation only if people know it's yours. Invisible work is a slow career death.

- Are you building systems others operate, or are you the recognised architect?
- When sending work for others to present, whose reputation are you actually building?

The expertise that makes you valuable can become the box that limits your growth.

Kavita's Strategic Expansion: From Specialist to Enterprise Leader

After seven years as the company's marketing expert, Kavita had built an enviable track record. Yet when the regional marketing director position opened, she wasn't even considered.

'Your expertise has become your cage,' her mentor explained. 'They see you as creative, not commercial.' It was true. In leadership meetings, Kavita was the 'brand person', sidelined during supply chain or P&L discussions. Her success had boxed her in.

That changed when the supply chain head mentioned struggling with vendor consolidation. Without overthinking, Kavita volunteered to lead it.

'That's not your area,' the COO said.

The supply chain head surprised everyone: 'She's managed dozens of agencies across regions. Maybe we need someone who thinks differently about vendor relationships.'

The first month was brutal. Unfamiliar spreadsheets. Hostile meetings. Stakeholders questioning why a 'brand person' was wasting their time. But instead of pretending to be an expert, she applied what she knew. She approached vendors like creative agencies. Segmented suppliers like consumer markets. Ran innovation workshops with packaging vendors.

Translation, not transformation.

Six months later, costs were down by 12%, onboarding time was halved and delivery rates reached 90%, with her supplier-relationship model becoming the regional standard. The COO who had doubted her now introduced her as 'our commercial leader who happens to have brand expertise'. When the director role reopened, Kavita got it.

'She proved she can lead beyond marketing,' the CEO explained. 'Creative thinking about operations and operational thinking about creativity are exactly what we need.'

Changing reputation required more than wanting different recognition; it meant taking real risks in unfamiliar territory and delivering unexpected value. Her supply chain success didn't diminish her brand expertise—it proved she could apply strategic thinking anywhere.

Pause and Reflect

Deep expertise establishes your value. It can also become your ceiling. The very thing that makes you indispensable can limit your progress.

- What specialised reputation is limiting your broader opportunities?
- Which unfamiliar territory could demonstrate range without abandoning core strengths?

You've seen how Arjun, Priya and Kavita transformed their reputations through transparency, visibility and range. But there's a reputation challenge that traps even successful managers: being seen as 'executional' rather than 'strategic'. This is the invisible ceiling most never break through.

What Your Boss Really Means When They Say 'Be Strategic'

'You need to be more strategic' remains the most common and least actionable feedback that middle managers receive. It creates a reputation ceiling for capable managers who deliver results, manage teams well and hit their targets, yet are not seen as leadership material.

The missing piece is not understanding what 'strategic' means to the people evaluating them. When senior leaders use this term, they are looking for three capabilities that signal readiness for broader roles.

1. Connect Work to Multiple Levels of Impact

Stop reporting only team metrics and start thinking and speaking at three levels. Consider all three in your decision-making, and then articulate the impact at each level when you brief leaders. The pattern is simple: team, organisation, industry.

For example, in a scenario with environmental clearances linked lending:

- *Team level*: 'We are meeting compliance requirements on this portfolio.'
- *Organisation level*: 'This reduces climate risk in our book and protects return volatility.'
- *Industry level*: 'This positions us for the shift to sustainable finance and future policy incentives.'

What to do: Frame every update with one sentence for each level. If you cannot state the organisational or industry effect, the work is not yet strategic or the story is incomplete.

2. Anticipate Beyond the Obvious Horizon

Operational managers react to today. Strategic leaders prepare for tomorrow. They prepare for multiple scenarios. They identify emerging patterns. They position teams for what's next, not just what's now.

The difference shows in how you frame discussions. Instead of 'here's how we'll hit Q3 targets', try 'here's what winning looks like next year and how this quarter builds towards it'.

That shift signals you're thinking beyond deadlines.

3. Lead with Outcomes, Not Process

Strategic thinkers know big ideas die in detailed presentations.

Never say, 'We're implementing a new lending platform with these features.' Always say, 'This turns compliance from a cost centre into a revenue driver.'

Start with business impact. Explain mechanics only when asked. Being strategic doesn't mean abandoning execution or speaking in abstractions. It means connecting your work to bigger outcomes and making that connection visible. This shift in framing becomes the foundation for a leadership reputation that opens doors.

Up Next: The Frameworks to Build Your Leadership Brand with Intention

You've seen how leadership brands emerge through critical moments and daily choices. But hoping people notice your work isn't a strategy; you need frameworks for that. The next chapter gives you these frameworks to build your brand deliberately: systems to assess perception, close reputation gaps and create visibility that accelerates your career.

Time to stop being accidentally good and start being intentionally visible.

14

The Reputation Architect

Most managers think great work will get noticed on its own. The three frameworks in this chapter address the issues that keep capable managers invisible: doing excellent work no one sees, being typecast into limiting boxes and stumbling in critical early moments.

Let's fix that systematically.

> **Frameworks in this chapter**
>
> **Three-Layer Amplifier**
> Purpose: Position your work, own the narrative and secure validation.
>
> **Adjacent Plays**
> Purpose: Stretch your range into near spaces without losing credibility.
>
> **30-60-100 Blueprint**
> Purpose: Learn fast, synthesise insights and deliver visible outcomes in three beats.

Framework 1: Three-Layer Amplifier (Positioning, ownership, validation for visible work)

Excellent work hidden in shadows serves no one, least of all your career. This framework ensures your contributions are seen and valued without appearing self-promotional. Visibility isn't about credit-grabbing. It's about strategic communication.

Your work's impact depends on who knows about it, understands its value and can act on it.

Layer 1: Strategic Positioning

Reframe your work to match organisational priorities. Reframe your operational improvements as risk mitigation initiatives, cost savings as increased investment capacity and efficiency gains as competitive advantages. Team development then becomes succession planning.

For example, don't say 'reduced processing time by 30%'. Say 'created capacity for 20% more customer transactions without additional investment'. Same work. Very different perception.

Layer 2: Narrative Ownership

Control how your contributions are packaged and delivered.

In-person: Convert data into stories. Replace fifty-page reports with five-slide presentations you deliver. Schedule skip-level meetings. Document methodologies so others cite you as a source.

Digital: Align your LinkedIn presence with your internal reputation. Share frameworks you've developed, lessons from projects you've led and perspectives on industry trends. Engage with leaders' posts thoughtfully. Comment on relevant discussions in your field. Remember that screenshots circulate and casual messages shape perception.

The goal: your thinking becomes as visible as your output.

Layer 3: External Validation

Internal visibility has ceilings. No matter how well you perform, only so many people inside your organisation will ever see your work. Your boss' boss might know you're good, but the CEO likely doesn't. Regional leaders outside your function probably haven't heard your name. External recognition changes this equation. When outsiders vouch for you, insiders see you differently.

Industry conferences where you represent the organisation create credibility that travels back to headquarters. Professional publications that showcase your expertise position you as a thought leader. LinkedIn content that reaches beyond your company expands your influence across your industry. Cross-company benchmark groups and advisory boards expand your network and multiply your visibility.

When external sources validate you, internal stakeholders notice. The marketing director known for speaking at industry events gets different consideration for strategy roles than equally capable peers who stay invisible

The Visibility Audit: List five significant contributions from the past year.

For each, document:

- Who knows about it (internally/externally)
- Who benefited directly
- Who could benefit but doesn't know.

This gap analysis reveals untapped visibility opportunities.

Making It Work: Choose one contribution. Elevate it through all three layers.

Track the difference between properly visible work and work that 'speaks for itself'. The contrast will convince you that visibility strategy matters as much as work quality.

Framework 2: Adjacent Plays (Stretch your range without losing credibility)

Being exceptional at one thing often becomes the cage that limits your growth.
This framework helps you strategically expand your reputation without abandoning core strengths. The goal isn't becoming someone different. It's demonstrating that your capabilities extend beyond current perceptions.
Strategic range enhances rather than dilutes your value.

Step 1: Map Your Reputation Box

Before expanding, define your current boundaries. Document what others actually think of you, not what you wish they thought.
Diagnostic questions:

- What projects automatically come to you?
- How do people introduce your expertise?
- Which opportunities never come your way?

If you're the 'operations expert', you never see strategy projects. If you're the 'creative type', you're excluded from P&L discussions.
These patterns reveal your box's walls.

Step 2: Choose Adjacent Territory

Expansion works best in complementary spaces, not contradictory ones. Evaluate potential areas against four criteria. Is it critical but underserved? Adjacent but different? Visible enough to be noticed? Challenging enough to change perceptions? The sweet spot: territory others wouldn't expect you to enter, but where your perspective unlocks unexpected value. For example, an operations expert taking on customer experience, bringing process discipline to marketing chaos.

Step 3: Design Undeniable Proof Points

Reputation expansion requires proof so compelling that others reconsider their assumptions. Strong proof points have measurable outcomes that matter. They show visible struggle and a genuine stretch. They bring novel approaches only you would think of. They earn endorsement from outside your usual sphere.

Small wins get dismissed as flukes. Substantial wins become reputation builders.

The Expansion Protocol: One strategic expansion per year. More than this dilutes focus.

- *Before starting*: Get sponsorship from someone credible in that space.
- *During expansion*: Document your learning journey transparently.
- *After success*: Connect new capability to core strengths.

Show how range makes you more valuable, not less focused.

Making It Work: Map your reputation box through three conversations with trusted colleagues.

Ask directly: 'What am I known for?' and 'What am I not considered for?' The answers will surprise you. Choose your first expansion carefully, as failed attempts reinforce the box rather than break it.

Remember: subsequent expansions become easier as others learn to see your range.

Framework 3: The 30-60-100 Blueprint (Learn, synthesise and deliver across three phases)

Your first hundred days in any role create lasting impressions that become surprisingly difficult to change. This framework transforms those crucial early days from anxiety-inducing trials into strategic reputation-building opportunities. Reputation forms through accumulated signals, not grand gestures.

The hundred-day mark is when temporary impressions solidify into permanent perception.

Phase 1: Days 1–30—Establish Your Learning Stance

Your first month signals judgement through the way you gather and weigh information. Teams notice which questions you ask, whose voices you include and how you handle conflicting data. The actions below matter because they show that your conclusions will rest on a complete picture rather than on first impressions or prior playbooks.

Key actions: Map all stakeholder perspectives before forming opinions. Ask second-order questions that reveal systems thinking. Seek dissenting voices, not just supporters.

Reputation signal: 'This leader thinks before acting.'

Warning: Arriving with ready solutions signals arrogance. Even if you've seen similar problems, demonstrating curiosity beats demonstrating knowledge.

Phase 2: Days 31–60—Reveal Your Thinking Process

In the second month, the focus shifts from absorption to synthesis. Show how you process information. How you weigh trade-offs. How you form hypotheses without making major changes yet.

Key actions: Share emerging mental models transparently. Present hypotheses as experiments, not verdicts. Acknowledge unknowns alongside insights.

Reputation signal: 'This leader combines clarity with humility.'

Warning: Keeping your thinking hidden creates anxiety. Teams need to see your reasoning evolve, not just receive polished conclusions.

Phase 3: Days 61–100—Deliver Selective Proof

The final phase requires targeted action. Choose initiatives significant enough to matter but contained enough to complete.

Key actions: Fix one broken system everyone notices daily. Deliver one unexpected win. Build one coalition that didn't exist. Establish one ritual that will outlast your tenure.

Reputation signal: 'This leader creates lasting value.'

Warning: Attempting everything signals poor judgement. Strategic focus beats hyperactive intervention.

The Feedback Loop

Day 30: Quietly ask three trusted advisors about how you're being perceived across the organisation and what reputation you're building.

Day 60: Test whether intended signals match received impressions.

Day 100: Lock in the perception you want to last.

Course-correct early. Impressions solidify fast.

Making It Work: Before starting any role, map your strategy:

- Ten stakeholders to engage in Phase 1
- Three systems to diagnose in Phase 2
- Two potential quick wins for Phase 3

First impressions last. Make them count.

Hold this plan lightly. What you learn in Phase 1 should reshape Phases 2 and 3. The framework provides structure, not a script. Reputation compounds as early signals get amplified through organisational networks. Those early signals become the filter through which everything else gets interpreted.

Let me share one final truth about leadership reputation that no framework fully captures.

The Price of Building Leadership Reputation: Turning Crisis into Credibility

During my two years as country GM in Sri Lanka, I faced a decision that would define how others saw my leadership capability. The Sri Lankan rupee crashed 60%, reducing my compensation to less than I'd earned as a middle manager. I was leading through cascading crises: COVID, economic collapse, fuel shortages preventing my team from reaching work.

The financial math said leave. The reputation calculus said stay, but only if I made the experience visible and positioned it strategically.

Here's what I learnt about reputation building during that period. I made my crisis leadership visible beyond Sri Lanka. I didn't suffer in silence. I shared lessons learnt at regional forums. I wrote about managing teams through extreme volatility. I presented case studies on maintaining performance when systems collapse. Each presentation positioned me as someone tested in conditions most managers only read about. I documented the capability growth, not just the hardship.

Rather than framing it as 'I stayed despite financial loss', I positioned it as 'I gained compressed leadership experience that normally takes a decade'. The narrative shifted from sacrifice to capability acceleration.

I let stakeholders see the full picture. When the opportunity to leave arose after stabilising operations, I considered it openly. I discussed trade-offs with regional leadership. The decision to stay became strategic, not stubborn. That visibility made the choice more impactful than silent endurance would have been.

The reputation benefit came from how I positioned the experience, not from the sacrifice itself. At regional meetings, leaders knew the specific capabilities I'd built maintaining team motivation through salary collapse, managing supply chains during infrastructure failure, leading when personal stakes were highest. When opportunities for broader roles emerged, decision-makers saw tested leadership capability. The difference mattered.

Reputation isn't built in your best moments but in your hardest choices. In Sri Lanka, I made that choice by measuring success in capability gained rather than money earned. The rest of my career would be defined by this decision.

That experience taught me that leadership reputation has a price tag most are not willing to pay. You cannot optimise for both comfort and credibility, and you cannot build a reputation for resilience without being tested. What I lost financially, I gained in unshakable credibility. When I speak about leading through volatility, people listen because they know I've lived it. When I advise on managing crisis, my words carry weight because everyone knows the price I paid for that knowledge.

Every leadership lesson has a price tag, and the most powerful ones, those that convert managers into leaders, never come at a discount. So, when the lesson shows up, be willing to pay the full price.

Common Reputation Traps to Avoid

The Perfectionist's Paradox: Waiting for perfect conditions before acting feels responsible but signals indecision. Your reputation suffers more from inaction than from imperfect action that you adjust along the way. Move, then improve.

The Invisible Excellence Trap: Assuming that excellent work speaks for itself is career limiting. Excellent work without visibility doesn't build reputation. Be good, then, be seen.

The Premature Expansion Error: Trying to be known for everything before being known for something dilutes your reputation. Establish one strong reputation anchor before adding new stories. Build depth in the area where your work already creates outsized results, then broaden from that base.

The Self-Promotion Backlash: Visibility is not the same as 'the work speaks for itself'. Make the outcomes and their impact visible through clear attribution, decision memos and short case walkthroughs, and keep the focus on the problem solved and the value created rather than on yourself. You are curating evidence so others can see the work, not campaigning for applause.

Signalling Leadership Readiness

Senior leaders evaluate reputation through specific signals:

Strategic thinking: You connect work to organisational priorities without prompting. You show understanding beyond immediate responsibilities. You see the system, not just your piece.

Coalition building: You earn trust and drive outcomes through influence, not position. You operate effectively in complex matrix structures. You create allies without authority.

Graceful recovery: You own failures without excuses. You extract lessons publicly. You turn mistakes into organisational learning.

Visible development: You create success stories beyond yourself. You scale impact through people, not just personal effort. Your team's growth proves your leadership.

Strategic expansion: You move beyond comfort zones in ways that serve organisational needs. You demonstrate the adaptability required for senior roles. You grow where the business needs you to grow.

The path from middle management to leadership isn't about years of experience or team size. It's about building a reputation that signals you can handle complexity, drive value across boundaries and elevate others while delivering results.

15

View from the Top with Vinita Vasanth

Vinita Vasanth is managing director and life sciences commercial practice lead for growth markets at Accenture.[1] *She sees reputation building from two angles: watching mid-level consultants navigate their own career progression, and seeing this play out in the client organisations she advises. That dual perspective makes her insights particularly valuable. She knows what works when building reputation inside a professional services firm, and she sees which behaviours her clients reward when promoting their own talent.*

Here's what she had to say.

Career progression is marked by pivotal milestones. The transition from individual contributor to team manager. Eventually, being recognised or hand-picked for formal leadership roles. These moments are more than title changes. They're opportunities to define your leadership style, demonstrate your values and show your ability to develop others.

In the early stages of management, clarity on performance expectations matters. So does the balance between support and freedom to achieve them. Hitting these metrics is baseline hygiene, necessary for progressing in any corporate environment. But true leadership goes beyond numbers.

---

1   See 'Vinita Vasanth', LinkedIn, https://www.linkedin.com/in/vinita-vasanth-80b51b4/.

It's about attitude, engagement, risk management and emotional intelligence; the ability to identify and harness strengths within a team while helping individuals develop skills they lack. A key indicator of leadership potential is how you adapt to change and respond to challenges, owning failures while sharing successes. That reflects humility and accountability.

Leadership reputation is twofold. It depends on how your team perceives you and how senior leadership views your impact. Both perspectives require deliberate, consistent effort to build and sustain. This isn't something that happens accidentally. You have to prioritise it and maintain it over time.

From my experience, shaping my leadership style involved exposure to diverse leadership approaches. I selected elements that resonated with my personality and learnt from strong mentors. Those conversations helped me develop a conscious and deliberate approach to leading teams.

An aspect often overlooked by aspiring leaders is understanding how their current managers can advocate for their careers. Many limit their efforts to their immediate supervisor. This constrains visibility and opportunities. The question to ask yourself is, 'How many voices will advocate for me in critical discussions?' That reveals gaps in advocacy you need to address.

I've seen talented managers plateau because they assumed their direct manager alone could champion their advancement. When that manager moved on or lacked influence in certain forums, they had no other advocates. The managers who advance fastest cultivate multiple sponsors across functions and levels. They make their work visible to leaders beyond their reporting line. They contribute to initiatives that put them in front of different decision-makers. This isn't politics. It's strategic relationship building.

The most effective way to build these advocacy relationships is through demonstrated impact. When you solve problems that matter to the business, people remember. When you help other teams succeed, they speak up for you later. When you handle crises with composure, senior leaders take note. Your reputation becomes the sum of these moments across multiple stakeholders.

Ultimately, the foundation of strong leadership reputation rests on several elements:

- The respect, response and reputation you earn from your teams
- Your ability to foster multiple voices that advocate on your behalf
- How effectively you handle and learn from risks or failures
- The empathy and human side you bring to the workplace
- The authenticity you demonstrate through your actions, achievements and leadership presence

16

Do-It Notes: Your Reputation-Building Road Map

Now it's time to systematically build your reputation. Start with reality, not wishful thinking. What are you actually known for today? How do you evolve that into what opens doors tomorrow? The gap between those two answers is your road map.

Build Before You Need It

'It takes twenty years to build a reputation and five minutes to ruin it. If you think about that, you'll do things differently.'
—*Warren Buffett*

Do-It Notes

This Month: Decode Your Current Reputation

1. *Conduct a reputation audit.* Ask five people across different levels: 'What am I known for?' and 'Which projects do you immediately associate with me?' Map the patterns. The gap between what you hear and what you intended reveals where to begin.

Do-It Notes: Your Reputation-Building Road Map 127

2. *Review your decision trail.* Examine five recent, visible decisions. What did you choose when facing trade-offs? How quickly did you act under pressure? Who did you protect or expose? These patterns reveal your actual leadership brand, not your imagined one.
3. *Assess your visibility gaps.* List three major achievements from the past year. For each of them, ask: who knows about it? Who should know but doesn't? Where did your contribution become invisible? This reveals the areas in which even excellent work isn't building reputation.
4. *Start your hundred-day plan.* If you're in a new role, map your approach. Month one: identify ten stakeholders to engage. Month two: diagnose three systems. Month three: deliver two quick wins. Structure prevents drift.

This Quarter: Build Your Reputation Foundation

1. *Claim your narrative space.* Stop delegating your insights. Present one major analysis yourself this quarter. Choose work with counter-intuitive findings that need your voice. Schedule two skip-level meetings. Share strategic thinking directly with decision-makers.
2. *Pick one strategic expansion.* Choose an area adjacent to your current perceived expertise/experience. Volunteer for one project outside your comfort zone. Apply your expertise to unfamiliar problems. Success here forces others to reconsider their assumptions about your range.
3. *Establish your learning brand.* Share one lesson learnt from failure each month in team meetings, leadership forums or internal posts. Ask for feedback publicly. Show how you're applying it. Vulnerability makes growth credible.
4. *Apply the Visibility Strategy.* Choose one significant contribution you have made. Position it in the context

of organisational priorities. Own its narrative instead of letting others present it. Seek external validation through conferences or LinkedIn. Track the difference between visible work and work that 'speaks for itself'.

This Year: Scale Your Reputation Systematically

1. *Create external validation.* Apply to speak at one industry conference. Write two articles for professional publications. Join one cross-company benchmark group. When external sources validate you, internal stakeholders notice differently.
2. *Build signature moments.* Design one reputation-defining experience. Lead a high-visibility crisis response. Turn around a failing project others avoided. Bridge a major organisational divide. These stories will define your leadership brand for years to come.
3. *Document your range.* Create proof points across three dimensions. Different functions (e.g. operations to strategy). Different contexts (e.g. growth to turnaround). Different approaches (e.g. analytical to creative). This breaks you out of limiting reputation boxes.
4. *Develop your leadership thesis.* Write your one-page philosophy. What do you uniquely bring to the company? Which problems can only you solve? What leadership gaps do you fill? This becomes your north star for reputation building.
5. *Build reputation advocates.* Nurture five people whose success reflects your leadership. Earn three senior sponsors who speak for you when you're absent. Generate two client testimonials for internal use. Others' success becomes a testament to your credibility.
6. *Track reputation metrics.* Monitor evolution through meeting invitations to strategic discussions you weren't

previously included in, requests for your expertise from other divisions, mentions in conversations you weren't part of and assumptions leaders make about your next role.

The Non-Negotiables

Three practices that compound reputation over time. Unlike the annual initiatives above, these become part of your weekly operating rhythm.

- *Weekly: The visibility check (Fifteen minutes)*
  Review where your work became invisible this week. Did someone else present your analysis? Did your framework get used without attribution? Did a meeting happen where your contribution should have been mentioned but wasn't?
  Course-correct immediately. Send that follow-up email. Schedule that presentation. Claim your narrative before someone else shapes it. Visibility doesn't happen automatically—it requires deliberate maintenance.
- *Monthly: The narrative claim (One hour)*
  Personally present one significant piece of work. No delegation. No proxies. This isn't about feeding your ego, but about ensuring decision-makers see your thinking process, not just your output.
  Choose work that demonstrates strategic capability, not just execution excellence. Show how you approached the problem, not just what you delivered. This is where leadership perception gets built.
- *Quarterly: The expansion push*
  Launch one initiative outside your current reputation box. If you're known for operations, lead a strategy project. If you're the analytical expert, take on something creative. If you're the Asia specialist, contribute to a global initiative.

Each quarter, add one piece of evidence that you're more than your label. This systematic range-building prevents you from getting stuck in a specialist box even as you deepen expertise.

You'll know it's working when:

- Skip-level leaders know your work without introduction
- You're invited to meetings above your level
- People seek your expertise outside your domain
- Others copy your approaches
- Your name comes up for opportunities you didn't pursue

The ultimate signal? When reputation precedes you rather than follows you.

Up Next: Teams and Transformation at Scale

When you stop trying to be impressive and start aiming to be impactful, reputation stops being an act. It becomes a signal. Something that draws trust, sparks performance and shapes how others lead.

The next sections explore how that reputation becomes a magnet for talent, turning a group of individuals into high-performing teams with shared purpose. That becomes the foundation for delivering enterprise transformation.

Ready to build something bigger than yourself?

PART 3
IMPACT: Leading at Scale

VALU**ES**

Exceptional Teams

Team Excellence = Interdependence + Development + Accountability

In practice: Create growth paths that strengthen rather than deplete your bench. Nurture teams that get better as they scale.

Sustainable Transformation

Leading Change = Capability + Culture + Credibility

In practice: Build systems that outlast individual heroes, shift behaviours through environment design and deliver results that prove transformation was worth the disruption.

Section 5: Exceptional Teams: Building Leaders Who Build Leaders

At a Glance

Some teams deliver breakthrough outcomes. Others with stronger individual contributors barely meet expectations. What makes the difference?

This section shows how to transform capable professionals into high-performing teams through deliberate design of work, systematic development of capability and creation of culture where excellence becomes self-sustaining.

Along the way, you will learn how:

- I discovered the critical difference between sponsorship and mentorship. Both are essential for turning individual contributors into leaders who build their own high-performing teams.
- Arjun integrated two rival R&D teams after an acquisition. He reframed competition as co-creation, designing challenges that made combined expertise essential for breakthrough innovation.
- Priya reversed a talent exodus by redesigning development. She created advancement pathways that made staying more attractive than leaving.
- You'll master frameworks for team transformation: the Team Integration Framework, Talent Development System and Performance Culture Method to build teams where collaboration emerges from structure, not personality.

To build teams that scale your leadership, you need the structure, the systems and the culture that make high performance repeatable.

17

When Teams Transcend Individuals

What High Performance Looks Like: A Personal Lesson

In mid-2022, eighteen months into my role as Sri Lanka's country GM, everything that could go wrong did. The country hit 70% inflation annually, ran out of fuel and lacked dollars to clear shipments from the port. Our business model collapsed as currency devaluation made bank guarantees worthless. Yet we not only survived but thrived, not because of my leadership but because of what the team became when facing impossible circumstances.

Manoj Jayawardena, our finance director, didn't wait for instructions. He met daily with every banker in Colombo, securing whatever dollar reserves existed to clear medicines from the port. While competitors' shipments sat in containers, our medicines reached patients.

Ravinder Ratnayake, our compliance officer, ran scenario-planning sessions projecting weeks ahead, when even government officials had no clarity. Her insistence that maintaining confidence would keep headquarters' support helped keep supply lines open.

Nirupa Wijeratne, our HR leader, turned wellness check-ins into lifelines for struggling employees. She secured monthly rations when stores emptied, ensuring people could feed families while serving patients.

Tyrone Fernando and Prasad Magammana, our sales and brand heads, kept one mission clear: maintain product availability. They retained distributors when others fled, ensured availability when supply chains collapsed and provided continuity when nothing else was certain.[1]

What emerged wasn't crisis management but genuine high performance. The team stopped waiting for permission and started solving problems. Functional boundaries dissolved into collaboration. Individual metrics became irrelevant next to keeping medicines flowing. This is what true teamwork looks like.

Within two years, their capability became so visible that global companies began recruiting. Nirupa joined Coca-Cola as HR director. Manoj became CFO at Rockland Distilleries. Ravindi Ratnayake moved to regional compliance leadership in Bangkok. Three colleagues joined our London headquarters in global roles. The crisis had become their career accelerator.

Contrast this with typical Monday planning sessions: people defending turf, rehashing failures, checking email while physically present but mentally absent. That's not a team but individuals sharing a manager. High-performing teams compound capabilities, spot opportunities individuals miss and create solutions no single member could conceive. My Sri Lankan team had no superior resources or calmer conditions; instead, they had shared purpose that transcended individual goals and the psychological safety to act without permission.

---

1 See 'Ravindi Ratnayake', LinkedIn, https://www.linkedin.com/in/ravindiratnayake/; 'Tyrone Fernando', LinkedIn, https://www.linkedin.com/in/tyrone-fernando-7248653a/; 'Prasad Magammana', LinkedIn, https://www.linkedin.com/in/prasad-magammana-830791b9/; 'Manoj Jayawardena', LinkedIn, https://www.linkedin.com/in/manoj-jayawardena-rockland/; 'Nirupa Janaka Kumara', LinkedIn, https://www.linkedin.com/in/nirupa-janaka-kumara-9a676132/.

The crisis stripped away traditional tools like budgets, bonuses and promotions. What remained was what actually makes teams excel. Shared purpose that transcends individual goals. Psychological safety to act without permission. Distributed leadership that doesn't wait for hierarchy. These aren't nice-to-haves. They're the only things that matter when everything else fails.

Why Many Teams Don't Become Exceptional Ones

The gap between average teams and exceptional ones isn't talent, resources or even leadership. It's the presence or absence of three critical design elements.

First: Genuinely interdependent work. Most organisations create artificial team structures around work individuals could do alone. Then they wonder why collaboration feels forced. Make collaboration necessary, not nice-to-have.

Second: Development systems that strengthen the team. When your best people can only advance by leaving, you're building a talent pipeline for competitors. Create growth paths that keep talent while elevating it.

Third: Cultural accountability. When accountability flows only vertically through hierarchy, you get compliance. When it flows horizontally through peers, you get excellence. The team should police its own standards.

Arjun's Integration Challenge: When Rivals Become Co-Creators

When Arjun was eight months into leading product development, his boss handed him what he called 'a fantastic opportunity'. In reality, the company had acquired a smaller firm, and Arjun had the unenviable task of merging two research teams that had spent years as competitors.

Twenty scientists sat in his conference room, refusing to make eye contact across the divide. His twelve had spent three years on one approach, while the eight newcomers had taken a different path. Both groups assumed the merger meant picking winners and losers.

'Ninety days to make this work,' his boss had said. 'One team, or we start cutting people.'

The first meeting went predictably badly, with the teams sitting on opposite sides. When Arjun presented integration plans, the acquired team's lead interrupted: 'So we abandon three years of work?'

'Our product is further along,' Arjun's team leader countered.

'Further does not mean better,' someone muttered.

Within minutes, data flew like weapons, and after an hour of trench-digging, Arjun called a break.

That night, the research files revealed something crucial. His team's product showed excellent results but poor absorption. The acquired team had solved absorption but struggled with dosing. These weren't competing solutions but complementary pieces. The rivalry had blinded them to the opportunity.

Arjun changed his approach completely, gathering both teams with one question: 'What would we build, starting fresh today, knowing everything we collectively know?'

Silence followed; both teams had expected to fight for survival. 'I am not asking you to abandon your work,' Arjun said. 'What could we create that neither team could achieve alone?'

The acquired team's lead finally spoke: 'Their structure might work with our absorption technology.'

That cracked everything open. Territory defence transformed into possibility exploration. Hoarded data flowed freely. The technical challenge eclipsed the turf war. What started as rivalry ended as teamwork.

Within a month, the team had outlined a combined approach. Nine months later, they delivered something neither team had imagined: a product that outperformed both originals, creating an entirely new category. Former rivals became co-inventors on shared patents.

Arjun didn't force harmony or compromise. He made the work more compelling than the conflict. By asking what they could build together rather than whose work survived, he turned competition into creation.

Pause and Reflect

Collaboration happens when the work itself makes it necessary, not when leaders demand it. Real interdependence can't be mandated. It must be designed into the work itself.

- When facing competing factions, do you choose sides or reframe challenges?
- How might two competing teams be redirected into collaboration without dismissing what each values?
- If this collaboration produces breakout talent, what runway will you create so they grow here rather than look elsewhere?

Priya's Talent Paradox: When Excellence Becomes Exodus

Priya had built one of commercial banking's best teams, consistently delivering insights that shaped regional strategy. Yet she sat reading her third resignation letter in six months, this time from her best analyst, who was being poached by another bank. The pattern was predictable: she would develop someone exceptional, their work would gain visibility and, within months, they would leave. Her star relationship manager jumped to a competitor, and her creative strategist was lured away by a start-up.

'You're running the company's best talent development programme, but it's becoming a problem,' her regional director said. 'We can't sustain excellence if everyone keeps leaving.'

The irony hurt because she had invested in developing people as good leaders do, but now that success was killing team stability. Each departure meant weeks of recruiting and training, only to repeat the cycle.

Peers offered simple solutions. 'Keep your best people in the background where competitors can't find them.' But Priya knew limiting growth would destroy what made her team special. Hold back stars and they'll leave sooner.

After studying why people left, she discovered the real issue wasn't money or titles but that people believed growth required departure since the only way up seemed out. Based on this insight, Priya restructured development completely. She created internal rotations where team members led different areas every six months—analytics to strategy to client work. The analyst hungry for strategic experience got it without leaving.

This was growth that didn't cost you people.

She negotiated organisational partnerships so her people could take three-month assignments with other divisions, work cross-functional projects and represent the bank at conferences, gaining exposure and networks without changing jobs. Most importantly, she repositioned the team from a support function to an internal consulting group shaping strategy. Team members led executive presentations and owned client relationships. The visibility that once made them targets for poaching now came with influence, making staying worthwhile.

Within a year, attrition dropped from 35% to 20%, and new talent sought her out, saying 'this is where future leaders are

When Teams Transcend Individuals

built', while performance improved as institutional knowledge accumulated and complex projects moved faster with seasoned teams.

'You've solved the talent paradox,' her director said. 'Your people are more valuable than ever but choosing to stay because growth here matches what they'd get elsewhere.'

Priya learnt that great teams do not prevent departures by limiting options; they create environments where staying offers better growth than leaving

Pause and Reflect

Retention isn't about locking people in. It's about giving them reasons to stay. Your best people need growth trajectories.

Are you developing people in ways that require departure?

When performers become restless, do you hold them back or stretch them forward?

Sometimes the problem isn't individual development but team accountability.

Up Next: The Frameworks to Build Teams That Multiply Impact

You've seen how strong teams get built through deliberate choices. Creating challenges that demand collaboration. Making growth visible. Shifting from self-focus to team elevation.

But hoping your team will gel isn't a strategy. The next chapter gives you frameworks to build high performance systematically

18
Teams That Grow Leaders

Most managers try to fix team problems through better hiring, clearer goals or stronger incentives. Those who build lasting excellence understand something different. Team performance is a design problem, not a people problem. Structure creates culture. Systems shape behaviour.

The three frameworks in this chapter transform team building from hope to a system.

> **Frameworks in this chapter**
>
> **Rivalry-to-Results**
> Purpose: Turn friction into co-creation with clear rules and shared wins.
>
> **Stay-and-Grow System**
> Purpose: Develop and retain talent through deliberate paths and visible progress.
>
> **Peer Accountability Code**
> Purpose: Set peer promises, reviews and consequences that sustain standards.

Framework 1: Rivalry-to-Results (Turn friction into co-creation with clear rules)

When groups are forced together through reorganisation, acquisition or project demands, the default outcome is dysfunction. This framework transforms competing factions into genuine collaborators. It makes interdependence essential rather than optional.

Stop forcing unity. Start designing necessity.

Step 1: Reframe from Competition to Co-Creation

Most integrations fail by asking which approach should win. This creates winners and losers. Instead, shift the conversation:

- Not 'Which approach should we adopt?' but 'What could we create that neither could achieve alone?'
- Not 'How do we merge these teams?' but 'What challenge makes collaboration more interesting than competition?'
- Not 'Who owns this?' but 'How does each group's expertise contribute to something bigger?'

This transforms zero-sum competition into positive-sum creation.

For example, two research teams with competing technologies may discover their approaches solve complementary problems. The challenge becomes creating a breakthrough neither could achieve independently.

Step 2: Design Genuinely Interdependent Work

Too many teams inherit a 'together on paper' structure while the real tasks can be done solo. People then coordinate out of habit rather than necessity, which is why collaboration feels staged.

Redesign the work so progress depends on combined strengths rather than parallel effort.

True integration needs four elements:

Distributed expertise: No single group holds all the skills or data required to move from problem to solution, so each team brings a non-substitutable piece.

- *Shared success metrics*: Outcomes are measured in a way that requires visible contributions from all parties, such as a revenue lift tied to both margin discipline and customer retention.
- *Compelling problem*: The challenge is ambitious enough that neither team can solve it alone, which makes cooperation the fastest route to impact rather than a governance ritual.
- *Time pressure with handoffs*: Deadlines and stage gates are set so one team's output is the other's input, making synchronised work more efficient than running in parallel.

When the analytical rigour of the finance team combines with the customer insight from marketing to solve what neither could crack alone, integration happens naturally.

Step 3: Build New Identity Through Shared Victory

Integration is complete when separate groups see themselves as one team. This happens through shared experiences of success impossible without collaboration. Create a unified identity by:

- Celebrating combined innovations over individual contributions
- Developing a shared language that blends both approaches
- Documenting the journey as team lore

- Promoting based on collaborative rather than individual achievements

Don't eliminate group identities. Create a superordinate identity that transcends them.

The Integration Protocol

Choose your pilot carefully. It needs to be important enough to engage top talent, but not so critical that failure would be catastrophic. Set aggressive timelines: eight weeks, not eight months. Teams should feel the pressure to skip political manoeuvring for practical progress. Measure what they create together, not how well they get along. Forced harmony produces compliance. Genuine interdependence produces innovation.

Making It Work: Identify two groups that should collaborate but don't. Map what each does well and where each struggles. Design a challenge that requires both. Set a six- to eight-week deadline for a tangible output.

Document what the integrated team produces that neither could create alone. This becomes your proof point for broader integration.

Framework 2: The Stay-and-Grow System (Develop and retain your best people)

Excellence is eroded when your best people leave just as they become valuable. This framework creates development architectures that strengthen rather than strip your bench. It makes staying as attractive as leaving.

Stop losing talent. Build a talent magnet instead.

Step 1: Map the Exodus Pattern

In exit interviews, employees often give sanitised reasons. Real understanding needs deeper investigation.

Action: Review three sources beyond HR scripts. Call two trusted ex-colleagues, analyse twelve months of internal mobility data and ask current team leads for the last two promotions they lost and why.

Common patterns behind departures:

- Growth appears to require leaving; promotions seem to come only by switching companies
- Expertise becomes constraining; being the 'expert' limits broader opportunities
- External visibility exceeds internal recognition
- Development feels like preparation for other companies

Document the pattern. Note when people leave, where they go, and what credible insiders say were the real reasons. The truth usually hurts, which is why it is useful.

Step 2: Design Internal Growth Paths

Create opportunities that advance scope and skill.

- *Rotation leadership*: Quarterly rotations where high-potentials lead different workstreams with clear deliverables, capability goals and decision rights.
- *Cross-division exposure*: Three-month secondments with adjacent divisions or markets, including at least one client-facing stint to bring back market context.
- *Teaching as development*: Training and mentorship assignments that build reputation while strengthening the team; teaching cements expertise and leadership credibility.

These must be real stretch opportunities with genuine authority, not token assignments.

Step 3: Build Matrix Navigation Capability

Your team faces the same competing priorities you do. Don't shield them. Build their capability to leverage complexity. When conflicting directives arrive, decode them together. Show the logic behind global mandates and the validity of local concerns. Teach them to package local innovations using corporate metrics.

Encourage network building before it's needed. The IT colleague becomes their transformation ally. The regional peer becomes their early warning system. When your people navigate organisational dynamics independently, they signal enterprise readiness while strengthening your reputation as a developer of leaders.

Step 4: Reposition the Team from Support to Strategic Engagement

The final shift changes how your team is perceived and valued. Move from providing analysis to shaping strategy. From supporting decisions to owning outcomes. From internal service to market-facing impact. From cost centre to value creator.

When your team becomes known as the place where future leaders develop, retention becomes organic. Ambitious people seek you out rather than leave.

The Development Protocol

Start with your highest flight risk, someone whose departure would genuinely hurt. Design a development plan providing what they would gain by leaving. New challenges. Increased visibility. Expanded networks. Different experiences.

Make this development visible to the entire team. Signal that growth doesn't require departure. Watch others request similar opportunities rather than update resumes.

Track not just retention but capability growth. Are people taking bigger challenges? Are they navigating complexity better? Are they developing others in turn?

Making It Work: Set up confidential conversations with three high performers about career aspirations. Listen for what would make them take other roles. Then fulfil that need internally. Every person you retain and develop becomes a magnet for other talent.

Create the virtuous cycle where your team becomes the place ambitious people want to be.

Framework 3: Peer Accountability Code (Peer promises, reviews and consequences)

Sustainable excellence requires cultures where high standards are maintained by peer accountability rather than managerial oversight. This framework establishes norms where the team polices its own performance. When teams own their standards, performance becomes intrinsic rather than imposed.

Stop being the enforcer. Start being the enabler.

Step 1: Establish Shared Standards

Performance cultures begin with explicit agreements about excellence, created by the team rather than imposed from above. Guide the team through defining:

- What does great look like in measurable terms?
- What minimum standards will we refuse to go below?
- Which metrics matter to us beyond management requirements?

For example, a development team may establish that no code goes live without peer review, critical bugs get fixed within twenty-four hours, technical debt never exceeds 20% of sprint capacity.

When standards come from within, enforcement becomes about integrity rather than compliance.

Step 2: Create Horizontal Accountability

Shift accountability from vertical hierarchy to horizontal peer relationships.

Peer review systems. Team members evaluate each other's work before external delivery. Catch issues early. Build collective ownership.

Buddy contracts. Pairs commit to each other's success. When someone struggles, their buddy intervenes before management notices.

Team retrospectives. Regular sessions without managerial presence. Honest conversations happen when the boss isn't watching.

Shared consequences. Structure rewards at the team level. When everyone wins or loses together, peer pressure becomes peer support.

The goal: Team members feel more accountable to each other than to management.

Step 3: Ritualise Continuous Improvement

Excellence is sustained through improvement habits built into team rhythms. Weekly learning forums where mistakes become teaching moments. Monthly capability assessments identifying skills to develop. Quarterly standard reviews raising the bar. Annual identity sessions reinforcing what makes this team exceptional.

Make improvement systematic, not exceptional.

The Culture Building Protocol

Start with one non-negotiable standard the team defines together. This may be response time, code quality or presentation polish. Have the team design how they'll hold each other accountable.

Expect initial discomfort. Team members will resist giving peer feedback. Push through and within weeks, peer accountability becomes more powerful than managerial oversight. Your role transforms from checking work to enabling systems.

Making It Work: Facilitate a session where your team defines one standard they won't compromise. Make it specific and measurable. Track the shift in your time allocation. Less quality control, more capability building. That's successful culture development.

When the team manages its own performance, you're free to focus on their growth.

The Power of Advocacy: A Personal Lesson in Building Others

Building exceptional teams ultimately requires investing in individuals with the same intensity that others once invested in you. Let me share a story that crystallised this for me.

Putting You in the Ring: What Sponsorship Looks Like

In late 2020, I was leading the commercial capability function for emerging markets for a global pharmaceutical company when I ran into Sridhar Venkatesh, our India managing director, at the office coffee machine. What started as casual conversation became career-defining.

'There's a country GM role opening in Sri Lanka,' Sridhar said. 'Small market, hundred people, but it's full P&L and would be a meaningful milestone.'

I had doubts. My background was commercial operations and capability building, not frontline sales or brand marketing typically required for general management. 'I don't have the typical profile,' I told him.

His response stayed with me: 'You're right. But you think in frameworks, connect dots and understand people. I'm putting you in the ring. The fight is yours to win or lose.'

Within weeks, my name was on the consideration list, though Sridhar did not guarantee the job, coach me through interviews or silence sceptics. He simply opened the door and ensured I had a shot. The process was rigorous, including psychometric tests, case presentations and four interview rounds, but I was in the ring.

That is sponsorship: someone using their capital to give you access to opportunities you have earned but might never reach otherwise.

Helping You Win the Fight: What Mentoring Looks Like

Once in the ring, I needed to perform, and this is where mentoring mattered. I reached out to Bhushan Akshikar, a regional leader who had run businesses across emerging markets and knew most decision-makers who would interview me. I expected a twenty-minute call with tips and encouragement.

Bhushan cleared his calendar. Over two forty-five-minute calls, he built my interview strategy. 'Round One tests financial acumen. Don't just discuss P&L: talk about cash flow and small-market realities. The regional lead values talent development, so have two examples ready. They'll probe distributor management, your weak spot. Here's how to reframe your background.'

Every detail mattered. He went further, emailing two panellists to vouch for me. I got the job; this time it was not just access but preparation. That is mentoring: deep investment, strategic guidance and real action.

Years later, I returned from Sri Lanka as VP of commercial excellence for the India business and Bhushan became the India MD, making my mentor my boss and completing the circle.

Sponsors create opportunity, using power to get you into rooms. Mentors help convert opportunity, investing time to build readiness. Most managers chase mentors while missing sponsors. But without sponsors, even prepared professionals miss opportunities that they're never considered for.

You need both. As you grow, be both for others. Put people in the ring. Then help them win.

From Receiving to Giving: Building Your Team Through Advocacy

In my first months as a newly promoted general manager, I wanted to prove my commitment to inclusivity. I nominated several women leaders on my team for a high-profile development programme. It was a multi-country women's leadership initiative, common in large global organisations. It offered masterclasses, one-to-one coaching and peer sessions—the full package. I ramped up my involvement with weekly check-ins, monthly group conversations and plenty of advice. I expected appreciation. Instead, I received useful feedback on my leadership behaviour.

During a debrief, my HR director, Nirupa Janaka Kumara, said, 'You coached the hell out of us, but we are over-coached and under-sponsored. We don't need as much advice as you think. What we need is for you to bring interesting roles to our table and talk about us in global forums. Please be a door-opener.'

I was embarrassed, and grateful. Coaching builds capability. Sponsorship moves careers. That conversation changed how I lead. I still invest in skill building, but I pair it with real advocacy: putting names forward for stretch roles, creating access to cross-functional work and speaking for people in rooms they're not yet in. This experience sharpened my distinction between mentoring, coaching and sponsorship. Mentoring and coaching prepare; sponsorship propels.

If you want to build high-performing teams, do both: develop and sponsor. Index less on advice, more on access. The leaders who advance others do more than guide; they open doors and keep them open long enough for people to walk through.

It's about becoming the advocate for your people that someone once was for you.

MENTORING ≠ COACHING ≠ SPONSORSHIP

Mentoring = Long-horizon, career-shaping guidance and context (what Bhushan did: strategy, framing the context for decisions, panel dynamics, sharing hard-earned wisdom).

Coaching = Skill/performance sharpening and cadence (what I gave the women leaders: weekly check-ins, group catch-ups, advice and actionable pointers).

Sponsorship = Door-opening with personal capital (what Sridhar did, and what Nirupa asked me to do more of). Speaking up for team members in promotion discussions.

What Gets in the Way of Team Excellence (And How to Fix It)

Five systemic blockers commonly derail team performance. Understanding why they emerge and how to address them prevents the slow slide into dysfunction. Most teams suffer from at least three. All five create mediocrity. Let's fix them systematically.

1. Role Ambiguity: The Accountability Killer

Role ambiguity creeps in during growth or reorganisation when 'we'll figure it out together' becomes the default. As a result, critical work falls through cracks. Tasks get duplicated. Meetings become process debates. Accountability evaporates because no one truly owns outcomes.

The fix: Create responsibility maps defining who decides, who executes, who gets informed. Update quarterly. Make them visible. When new projects arise, clarify roles before discussing deliverables. Upfront investment prevents downstream confusion.

2. Communication Breakdowns: Death by a Thousand Cuts

Communication doesn't fail dramatically. It erodes through skipped check-ins, unconfirmed assumptions, information hoarding. Digital tools worsen this. Critical updates get buried in chat streams. Important decisions are lost in overflowing inboxes. The situation is aggravated by remote work, which eliminates casual conversations that once allowed problems to surface early.

The fix: Design communication matching work patterns. Daily fifteen-minute stand-ups for complex collaboration. Asynchronous updates for distributed teams. Most critically, establish 'communication contracts' that include explicit agreements about response times, channels and escalation paths.

3. Trust Deficit: When Self-Protection Wins

Trust is eroded through small disappointments. Missed deadlines without warning. Credit taken for shared work. Confidences broken publicly. Teams respond to the trust deficit predictably: hoarding information, documenting defensively, avoiding vulnerability.

The fix: Rebuild through structured vulnerability. Publicly acknowledge mistakes. Ask for help. Share uncertainty. Create 'failure forums' for blame-free learning. Address violations immediately and visibly. Teams watch your response more than your words.

4. Skill Gaps: The Hidden Bottleneck

Teams face both technical gaps (missing expertise) and collaborative gaps (inability to work together). Work flows to the few team members with critical skills. Bottlenecks and burnout follow. Others feel underutilised and consequently disengage from the job. Team capacity becomes defined by the weakest link, not collective capability.

The fix: Conduct quarterly capability assessments. Map technical and collaborative skills. Identify single points of failure. Create redundancy through knowledge transfer. Institute skill-sharing sessions. Build bench strength before you need it.

5. Misaligned Incentives: Rewarding the Wrong Thing

Organisations praise teamwork while rewarding individual achievement. People know they should collaborate, yet their careers seem to depend on standing out. The result is that 'I' takes precedence over 'we'. Information gets hoarded. Visibility trumps value.

The fix: Include team metrics in individual reviews. Not just team success, but how individuals enabled others. Create 'assist' metrics tracking collaborative contribution. Celebrate team victories more than individual wins. When promoting, evaluate how candidates built capability in others.

These derailers interact destructively. Role ambiguity creates communication breakdowns. Breakdowns erode trust. Lost trust exposes skill gaps. Misaligned incentives prevent fixes. The dysfunction compounds.

Watch for warning signs: increasing coordination overhead, top talent requesting transfers, slower decisions despite clear processes, energy spent on internal politics rather than external competition. When you spot these signals, intervene immediately. Teams rarely self-correct from systemic dysfunction.

Signalling Leadership Readiness

Senior leaders evaluate team-building capability through specific signals:

Transform dysfunction into performance. Take underperforming groups and make them exceptional without wholesale replacement. Build with what you have, not just ideal resources.

Retain while developing. Create environments where top talent grows without leaving. Build bench strength rather than export talent.

Create self-sustaining excellence. Establish cultures that maintain high standards in your absence. Build systems, not dependencies.

Scale through others. Develop leaders who develop others. Show multiplication of capability, not just addition.

Handle complexity. Successfully integrate diverse groups. Manage matrix relationships. Build collaboration across boundaries.

Master these frameworks, and you transform from someone who manages talented people into someone who builds teams that redefine what's possible.

19
View from the Top with Vikas Dua

To understand what HR leaders look for while assessing leadership readiness on team excellence, I asked Vikas Dua, head of HR at Weber Shandwick.[1] *With more than twenty-five years of diverse experience spanning hospitality, education, IT-ITES and PR, Vikas has helped shape the careers of over 1,20,000 professionals across India. He is a LinkedIn Top Voice.*

Here's what he had to say.

What Defines Manager Readiness for Team Leadership

When evaluating managers for leadership roles, I look for those who build teams defined by shared purpose, deep trust and consistent accountability.

In my experience, the managers I've taken bets on create environments where team members operate with psychological safety. People feel free to speak up, challenge ideas and take ownership of results. These managers understand that success isn't just about hitting targets. It's about building collective resilience and a growth mindset that fuels innovation.

The best team builders I've seen embrace diversity in perspectives, help their teams learn rapidly from feedback and

---

1 See 'Vikas Dua', LinkedIn, https://www.linkedin.com/in/vikasdua/.

maintain constructive conflict for creative problem-solving. They create this environment through clarity, empowerment and continuous learning systems.

How Strong Managers Build Trust

Over the years, I've observed that managers who successfully transition to leadership understand that trust is built through transparency and consistency. They model both in their behaviours. They initiate open conversations about challenges, practise fair decision-making and recognise vulnerability to foster psychological safety. The most effective ones I've worked with establish regular trust check-ins or open retrospectives that normalise honest dialogue about what's working and what's not.

These managers lead with empathy and evidence, ensuring feedback is balanced and timely. What I've learnt is that they understand trust accelerates execution because it shortens hesitation and builds confidence in collective capability.

In the teams they build, trust becomes the currency of collaboration.

How They Set Goals That Create Alignment

The managers I've promoted to leadership begin with aligned purpose and SMART goals: specific, measurable, achievable, relevant and time-bound. They involve team members in goal-setting to build ownership and accountability.

They ensure that goals cascade from organisational priorities, keeping every individual's work visible and meaningful. They establish progress reviews and transparent dashboards that maintain a line of sight to results while celebrating milestones.

In my experience, the strongest managers balance clear metrics with flexibility, allowing teams to adjust when business realities shift. In these dynamic times, they continuously re-evaluate and reset goals, aligning each team member to new objectives.

How They Sustain Motivation Over Time

The managers I've seen build exceptional teams create sustained motivation through a mix of purpose, recognition and growth. Their teams thrive because people see how their work drives impact. These managers connect tasks to broader organisational goals, celebrate everyday wins and ensure meaningful professional development. They use recognition, both formal and peer-driven, to reinforce belonging, while development programmes fuel long-term engagement.

What I've observed is that they notice and nurture effort, not just output. Under their leadership, engagement becomes self-sustaining because people feel seen, stretched and supported.

How They Enable Continuous Performance

The managers I've backed for advancement embed feedback, learning and agility into daily operations. They move beyond annual reviews, using real-time coaching and learning interventions to keep teams adaptive. They champion skill audits, curated training and mentorship programmes that match growth needs with business strategy. They establish frequent feedback loops that ensure no one stalls or drifts.

In what I've witnessed across industries, these managers convert performance management from an event into a living culture, one where improvement is constant, learning is shared and excellence becomes habitual.

20

Do-It Notes: Your Team-Building Road Map

Now it's time to transform team-building insights into systematic practice. The core question isn't 'How do I manage my team better?'; it's 'How do I architect an environment where collaboration is natural, excellence is self-sustaining and growth strengthens rather than depletes the team?'

Stop managing people. Start designing systems.

Design Beats Desire

'Culture eats strategy for breakfast, but structure eats culture for lunch.'

—Anonymous

Do-It Notes

This Month: Diagnose Your Team Reality

1. *Map your collaboration patterns.* Track decisions requiring multiple people who don't naturally collaborate. Note where work gets stuck waiting for handoffs. Identify which

tasks need genuine teamwork versus forced collaboration. Reality often surprises you.
2. *Audit your talent flow.* Document the past eighteen months. Who left? Where did they go? Which capabilities walked out? Who stayed and what truly kept them? The pattern reveals your reputation.
3. *Assess accountability flow.* Do people only deliver when you're watching? Who holds others accountable without your involvement? Is performance maintained in your absence? Your answer determines your freedom.
4. *Identify integration opportunities.* Find two groups that should collaborate but don't. Map what each does well and where each struggles. The gap is your opportunity.

This Quarter: Build Team Architecture

1. *Design one genuinely interdependent challenge.* Create a project where success requires multiple perspectives. No individual has all expertise. A timeline makes collaboration more efficient than parallel work. Watch collaboration emerge from necessity instead of a mandate.
2. *Create internal growth paths.* Take your highest flight risk. Design a three-month stretch assignment for them that gives them growth and exposure within the organisation. Give them leadership of something meaningful with external visibility. Make their development visible to others.
3. *Establish peer accountability.* Have team members review each other's work before it reaches you. People then make commitments to teammates, not just you. Run one retrospective meeting without your presence. The team will start managing itself.

4. *Run an integration experiment.* Frame a challenge that requires the combined expertise of the two functions you need to align. For example, finance with marketing for customer acquisition, or R&D with manufacturing for scale-up. Set an eight-week timetable with shared milestones so slippage hurts both sides. Agree on two joint success metrics and one decision owner. Measure what they produce together and record the ideas that neither team could have delivered alone.

This Year: Scale Team Excellence

1. *Build your talent development architecture.* Create systematic growth through a quarterly rotation of leadership roles. Through this, senior members get the opportunity to teach. Everyone gets external partnerships. Track whether people take bigger challenges, navigate complexity better, develop others.
2. *Install performance culture rituals.* Put in place weekly learning forums where mistakes become teaching, monthly capability assessments, quarterly standard reviews that raise the bar. Make high performance self-sustaining, not manager-dependent.
3. *Document your methodology.* Capture your team design principles. Create playbooks for common challenges. Build templates others can use. Transform experience into transferable capability.
4. *Measure multiplication effects.* Track leaders produced by your team, innovations that scale beyond you, practices other teams adopt. Some specific targets you can have: 20–30% promoted annually, team members leading enterprise initiatives, former team members managing their own teams.

5. *Develop team leaders beyond your team.* Teach other managers your approaches. Share integration frameworks. Export your development model. Your impact should extend far beyond direct reports.

The Non-Negotiables.

Three practices that build team excellence:

- *Weekly*: The collaboration audit (fifteen minutes). Review where work requires genuine teamwork versus forced collaboration.
- *Monthly*: The talent conversation (thirty minutes). One development discussion with a high performer about their growth trajectory.
- *Quarterly*: The peer accountability check (one hour). Assess what the team self-regulates without your involvement.

These ensure you're building a team, not managing an arbitrary group of people.

You'll know it's working when:

- The team delivers excellence in your absence
- People choose to stay despite external opportunities
- Other teams adopt your practices
- Former team members become successful leaders
- Collaboration happens without orchestration

The ultimate test is whether your team performs just as well without you, and in critical moments even better. The benchmark is sustained outcomes, sound decisions aligned with intent and only rare escalations when stakes or scope truly require you.

Up Next

Your brand earns you the invitation. Your bench proves you deserve the bigger stage. Together, they're the foundation for leading transformation without losing your people, which is where we're headed next.

Section 6: Sustainable Transformation: Delivering change that sticks and scales

At a Glance

When disruption hits and playbooks fail, someone must step up. When systems break and cultures resist, someone must create the path forward. That someone could be you.

This section explores the shift from change participant to transformation architect. You'll learn to lead when there's no map, the stakes are high and your reputation depends on the outcome. Stop executing others' plans. Start building systems that work when traditional approaches fail.

Along the way, you will learn how:

- I led a market exit during Sri Lanka's worst economic crisis. Transformation requires building the village, not trying to be the hero who saves it alone.
- Arjun turned a small AI pilot into a digital blueprint and cut drug development timelines by 20% by understanding that trust enables transformation, while technology merely supports it.
- Priya reimagined banking from product push to platform play. She reduced customer acquisition costs by treating digital disruption as an opportunity to redesign relationships.
- Kavita led an operational revolution cutting environmental footprint by 20%. She transformed sceptical stakeholders into co-creators, turning a compliance burden into competitive advantage.

You'll master practical transformation tools. Build early momentum in your first hundred days, accelerate adoption across resistant cultures and sustain change beyond the initial push.

To lead enterprise change, you need the skills to scale, the culture to sustain it and the trust to bring people with you.

21

Building the Transformation Muscle

Your inbox holds four versions of the same project plan, all different. Before you can identify and correct the discrepancies, you're pulled into a crisis call about a tech rollout that has paralysed frontline teams. During a one-on-one, your direct report says, 'We're doing everything asked, but nothing's changing.'

Welcome to transformation in its messiest form. You're told to 'drive change' without anyone explaining what that means inside a moving business. You're expected to maintain operations while redesigning them. Hold trust while dismantling familiar systems. Project confidence when the destination remains unclear.

This is the transformation paradox.

Most middle managers get stuck here because they confuse transformation with execution. They think it is about rolling out new systems or hitting different KPIs, when it is about helping people believe in what is next while building the bridge to get there. Those who break through understand that transformation isn't a project you manage but a capability you build. They know how to create momentum when resistance peaks and maintain credibility when early attempts stumble.

Transformation rarely arrives with a formal invitation or a clear mandate. It usually starts when something breaks and the usual fixes stop working. When market shifts make current models obsolete. When technology disrupts faster than organisations can adapt. The question isn't whether transformation will find you. It's whether you'll be ready.

Middle managers who advance don't wait for perfect conditions or complete authority. They recognise transformation moments and step into them.

Leading transformation requires three critical capabilities:

- *Building while flying*: Creating new systems while maintaining current operations
- *Translating resistance*: Converting scepticism into co-creation
- *Scaling through trust*: Keeping change alive through culture when rules can't

Get good at these, and transformation starts speeding up your career.

Leading a Business Exit During Crisis: A Personal Lesson

Towards the end of 2022, as I prepared to transition from my role as country GM for Sri Lanka, headquarters delivered a mandate that would test everything I'd learnt about transformation. We were shutting down local operations and moving to a distributor model as part of global restructuring targeting smaller markets.

The timing couldn't have been worse. Sri Lanka was experiencing its worst economic crisis in history. Fuel shortages. Sky-high inflation. Political protests. Systematic breakdown of public services.

In this chaos, I had to shut down operations we'd run for decades, identify and onboard a distributor within ninety days, manage job losses for the committed local team and maintain medicine supply throughout.

There was no precedent for exiting a market in the middle of an economic collapse. Every decision felt like choosing between equally important values. Should we prioritise speed to minimise uncertainty or take time to find the right partner? Should we focus on employee support or business continuity? Should we maintain full transparency or manage information to prevent panic?

The experience taught me that transformation leadership requires wearing two hats simultaneously.

The Actor: Teams need emotional anchoring during transformation. How you show up in town halls, crisis calls and corridor conversations sets the tone. You become the steadiness others borrow when their world feels uncertain.

The Architect: While projecting stability, you're simultaneously building new models in real time. Making decisions with incomplete information. Structuring partnerships without precedent. Creating systems unlike anything your organisation has done before.

You must be both at once. What got us through wasn't strategy but collective leadership. My team's resilience, their commitment to doing right by patients and people and their ability to execute while everything shifted made transformation possible. We successfully transitioned to the distributor model while maintaining medicine supply, supporting displaced employees and preserving stakeholder trust.

That experience crystallised what transformation really demands. Making unpopular decisions while maintaining trust. Building the new while honouring the old. Staying human while being strategic.

Transformation isn't about answers. It's about living with contradictions. Transformation also looks different in each context, as Arjun, Priya and Kavita discovered. Each started where you might be now, caught between old models that no longer work and new ones that don't yet exist.

Arjun's Digital Transformation: The Human Side of Technology Change

'We're three years behind,' the global R&D head announced. 'Our competitors are using AI to cut drug development timelines by 30%. We need to move now, or we'll be irrelevant by 2028.'

Arjun inherited three research centres with hundred scientists who had zero enthusiasm for algorithms replacing intuition. His first town hall bombed when a senior researcher with twenty-five years at the bench interrupted: 'AI is hype. Real science happens in labs, not laptops.'

And it wasn't just sceptical scientists that Arjun was facing. IT teams obsessed over data integrity. Compliance leaders guarded validation protocols. Everyone had reasons to resist. Traditional change management would mandate adoption. Arjun recognised this as a trust challenge, not a technology problem.

He started with drug interaction mapping, a painful six-week manual process that AI could reduce to four days. He chose a respected but mid-level researcher for the pilot, someone sceptical but fair. The deal was simple: if it wasted time, they would stop.

Five days later, she called: 'The AI found three interactions I would have missed. I finished a month early.'

Rather than broadcasting success through emails, Arjun let her tell the story at the research forum. Three scientists volunteered for the next pilot. Then twelve. Then entire teams. Each success was reframed around what scientists actually cared about: testing more hypotheses, helping patients faster, creating time for creative research. Trust spread peer to peer, not top down. The change stuck because it didn't feel forced.

The digital notebooks looked like paper but synced worldwide. AI suggestions appeared as colleague input in familiar interfaces. Compliance was automated within workflows, not around them. Change happened quietly, almost unnoticed.

Six months in, AI-assisted modelling identified a promising compound that traditional screening had missed, potentially cutting development by two years. Scientists started forming AI journal clubs. They stopped fearing the system and started trusting it.

The breakthrough moment came when the original sceptic announced at the global summit: 'I was wrong. This isn't replacing science. It's making me a better scientist.'

Eighteen months later, drug development timelines were down 20%, approaching the competitive benchmark, and regulatory approvals became 30% faster. Scientists' identities had shifted from fearing obsolescence to seeing themselves as future ready.

Pause and Reflect

People adopt transformation when they trust it will make their work better, not when mandates force compliance. Trust beats technology every time.

- How do you lead change when you have responsibility but limited control?
- What makes people trust new tools versus resist them, even when the benefits are obvious?

Sometimes transformation requires reimagining your entire business model, not just adopting new tools.

Priya's Business Model Evolution: From Products to Ecosystems

Traditional banking was becoming invisible as customers no longer wanted standalone financial products. Instead, they asked for integrated solutions that simplified their entire business operations. As head of commercial banking strategy, Priya received a mandate to shift the bank from product-first to a platform-led ecosystem.

The competition was already ahead. Fintech start-ups offered slick single-purpose apps while global players embedded financial services into supply chains. Meanwhile, her product teams still tinkered with loan rates and fee structures as the market sprinted away.

Priya couldn't just launch a platform but had to redesign how the bank thought, worked and measured success without tanking quarterly numbers or triggering compliance alarms.

She started by mapping customer journeys. Small businesses didn't just need loans. They needed payroll tools, tax filing, invoice tracking, insurance bundling. Mid-sized corporates wanted ESG reporting, procurement support, cross-border financing.

The bank had trust, networks and risk intelligence. These could become the foundation of something bigger. So instead of pushing products, Priya built partnerships. Logistics platforms. HR software firms. Accounting tools. Specialised lenders. The bank became the orchestrator rather than provider. The trusted connector in a larger ecosystem. Platform thinking replaced product thinking.

Early pilots proved the model worked with bundled solutions driving 40% higher product penetration, reducing churn by 30% as customers found switching costs prohibitive once integrated into the ecosystem.

But success created a subtler challenge: narrative drift. Relationship managers still told clients 'We're a bank, not a tech company.' They thought they were being pragmatic. They were actually undermining the transformation. Old stories kill new strategies.

Priya made narrative discipline non-negotiable. Every leader had to reinforce the same message in client pitches and team meetings: 'We help you run your business better, not just your bank account.' Whether customers talked to managers in Mumbai or Singapore, they heard the same promise.

The transformation took eighteen months, with revenue from platform services growing from zero to 15% of commercial banking income. Customer satisfaction scores hit record highs as the bank went from losing market share to gaining it.

Pause and Reflect

Customers don't want your products. They want their problems solved. Transformation happens when you stop selling what you make and start solving what matters.

- Where are the early cracks in your industry's business model?
- What would it take to move from product provider to problem solver?

Sometimes transformation means rewiring operations when sustainability pressures expose supply chain vulnerabilities.

Kavita's Sustainability Transformation: When Marketing Drives Operations

Kavita's challenge didn't arrive as one dramatic crisis. It came as a pile-up of slow-burning ones. As regional marketing director for a top consumer goods company, she watched pressure mount from every side. Regulators tightening rules on emissions and packaging. Consumers demanding ethical products with transparent supply chains. Investors watching ESG metrics closely. Supply chains buckling under climate shocks and geopolitics.

The old playbook was dying.

Then the CEO announced a target to cut the environmental footprint by 25% in three years. Performance would not be sacrificed; they also had to lower costs, improve quality and build resilience. Kavita knew that if she treated sustainability as an add-on, it would get sidelined the moment targets slipped. She needed to integrate it, not as a CSR side project, but as part of her KPIs for quality, efficiency and cost.

Her first step was finding performance synergies, places where reducing environmental impact would also cut costs, improve quality or speed things up. Waste audits exposed hidden inefficiencies. Lightweight packaging cut costs and emissions. Switching to renewables lowered long-term OPEX after the upfront hit. Supplier partnerships led to shared goals, shared risks and better predictability.

Next came building the innovation muscle. She framed sustainability not as constraint but as a creative brief. Cross-functional teams were tasked with rethinking processes from scratch. Circular product design making recycling part of the value chain. Reverse logistics for take backs and reuse. Supplier partnerships sharing cost savings and ESG gains. Constraint became catalyst.

One packaging pilot cut plastic by 30% while also speeding up assembly line changeovers. The supply chain team started pitching sustainability ideas of their own.

To make it stick, Kavita needed systems-level integration. She built dashboards tracking financial, environmental and operational KPIs side-by-side. That visibility changed behaviour. Procurement saw the cost impact of emissions-reducing suppliers. Plant managers tracked how energy efficiency drove both OPEX savings and ESG scores. Marketing linked sustainability features directly to customer satisfaction. When you measure it together, you manage it together.

The tipping point came when sustainability started funding itself: a 20% reduction in environmental footprint and a 15% improvement in operational efficiency.

Pause and Reflect

Your functional expertise becomes most powerful when you use it to help others see possibilities they're missing. Marketing isn't just about messaging. It's about reframing reality.

- What market insight could reframe an operational constraint as competitive advantage?
- How could your functional expertise help other departments see transformation differently?

Up Next: The Frameworks to Make Transformation Repeatable

You've seen transformation through lived experience. Market exits during crisis. Resistance to new technology. Global mandates meeting local realities.

But hoping you'll figure it out under fire isn't a strategy. The next chapter gives you frameworks to assess organisational readiness, decode stakeholder dynamics and build change capability that becomes your competitive advantage.

22
The Transformation Architect

Most managers attempt transformation through sheer willpower, treating each initiative as unique, learning through expensive mistakes and burning out teams along the way. Those who lead sustainable change understand something different. Transformation requires systematic capability.

Diagnose readiness before launching. Build momentum that compounds. Embed change that outlasts leadership attention.

Frameworks in this chapter

CAP Assessment
Purpose: Gauge capacity, alignment and preparedness before committing to change.

The Four Forces of Momentum
Purpose: Drive purpose, progress, people and persistence to keep change moving.

The Sticky Change Protocol
Purpose: Lock outcomes with governance, routines and simple guardrails that last.

Framework 1: CAP Assessment (Capacity, Alignment, Preparedness)

When organisations launch transformations without understanding their true capacity for change, the default outcome is predictable: resistance, exhaustion, failure. This method reveals the hidden factors that determine whether your transformation will build momentum or hit walls.

Step 1: Map Organisational Change Capacity

Most transformations treat organisational capacity as infinite. It's actually like working memory with finite bandwidth that degrades under overload.

Map your organisation's true capacity:

- What changes are already consuming attention?
- Where has change fatigue set in versus where energy remains?
- Which functions have bandwidth versus which are stretched thin?
- How did previous changes succeed or scar the organisation?

When three system upgrades, two restructures and a merger are already underway, even brilliant strategies struggle for oxygen. Design for actual capacity, not theoretical readiness.

Step 2: Assess Stakeholder Readiness

Stop treating stakeholders as a monolithic group to be 'brought along'. Different stakeholders need fundamentally different engagement strategies. Map them across two dimensions: ability to accelerate or block change, and current readiness to embrace transformation.

This reveals four groups:

1. *High-influence champions*: Your early coalition and trusted voices
2. *High-influence sceptics*: The ones who need proof through results, not presentations
3. *Eager supporters*: The ones with less formal power but who spread success stories organically
4. *Low-influence resistors*: Who shouldn't consume disproportionate early energy

Track movement over time. When sceptics shift to being neutral or neutrals become advocates, transformation is gaining authentic traction.

Step 3: Evaluate Implementation Complexity

Transformation complexity isn't binary but multidimensional. Understanding true complexity prevents you from treating complex transformations like simple ones. Through this, you avoid expecting speed when you need patience and assuming alignment when you need orchestration.

Assess complexity across five factors:

1. Technical integration requirements across systems
2. Number of functions that must coordinate
3. Process interdependencies creating cascading impacts
4. Magnitude of behavioural change required
5. External pressures: timeline, competition, regulation

Facing high complexity doesn't mean you have to abandon transformation. It means designing differently. Simple transformations can sprint with focused teams. Complex ones require patient orchestration, extensive infrastructure and explicit coordination.

The Readiness Protocol: Run this audit with your leadership team. This will help you identify gaps between perspectives, which reveal blind spots in your strategy. For example, when finance sees low resistance but operations sees high complexity, this is a critical misalignment. Resolve it before launch.

Update your strategy monthly as conditions shift. Initial resistance may soften after early wins. Apparent simplicity in the system may reveal hidden complexity once implementation begins.

Share results strategically. Full transparency with your core team. Selective sharing with broader audiences who need confidence, not complexity.

Making It Work: Map one transformation you're currently planning or leading. Document what's already changing in your organisation. Identify ten critical stakeholders and their positions. Assess complexity across all five factors.

Then design your approach to match reality:

- Choose battles based on actual capacity
- Engage stakeholders based on actual position
- Structure rollout based on actual complexity

This shift from wishful planning to reality-based design determines whether transformation energises or exhausts the organisation.

Framework 2: The Four Forces of Momentum (Purpose, Progress, People, Persistence)

Most transformations start with energy and end with exhaustion. Leaders tend to focus on launching change rather than sustaining it. This often leads to momentum fizzling out before the desired change is achieved.

This method creates self-reinforcing momentum that grows stronger over time rather than degrading through organisational friction. Don't push change; make people want to move.

Step 1: Create Purpose Beyond Performance

Most transformations lead with efficiency metrics when people need meaning to sustain difficult change. Organisations don't transform for 10% improvements. They transform for purposes that elevate daily work into meaningful contribution.

Connect transformation to purpose. Highlight:

- Human impact beyond financial returns
- Competitive advantage ensuring survival
- Legacy outlasting quarterly results
- Problems worth solving despite difficulty.

When digital transformation means 'faster access to life-saving treatments' rather than 'operational efficiency', resistance transforms into urgency. Find authentic connection, not manufactured inspiration.

Step 2: Design Phased Victories

Momentum dies when progress feels theoretical and victories seem distant. To avoid this trap, architect escalating wins that build confidence while delivering value. Make each phase easier than the last, not harder.

Structure your transformation:

- *Pilot victories*: Prove possibility without risking everything.
- *Expansion wins*: Show scalability beyond special circumstances.

- *Integration successes*: Demonstrate sustainability.
- *Transformation completion*: Deliver the full vision.

Each phase delivers tangible value within ninety days. The pilot provides proof of concept. Expansion proves scale. Integration proves durability. Completion proves transformation.

Celebrate progress without declaring premature victory.

Step 3: Build Coalition Architecture

Transformation through individual heroics exhausts leaders and creates dependency. Sustainable momentum requires distributed leadership with maintained coherence.

Create four coalition layers:

- *Core team*: They own transformation day to day.
- *Champions*: They advocate for change and remove barriers in the way.
- *Early adopters*: They prove that the change works.
- *Amplifiers*: They spread success stories organically.

The design matters more than any one person. Well-designed coalitions survive personnel changes. Poor ones collapse when key people leave. Give real authority, not ceremonial involvement.

Step 4: Establish Narrative Discipline

Transformation momentum is eroded when different leaders tell different stories. Mixed messages create confusion, which resistant elements will exploit. Healthy scepticism becomes active opposition.

Maintain narrative consistency through these measures:

- One core message every leader reinforces
- Multiple supporting stories that illustrate, not contradict, your narrative
- Regular communication cadence preventing rumours
- Two-way dialogue bringing concerns to the surface, not suppressing them

Whether someone talks to a frontline supervisor or senior executive, they should hear the same fundamental story. Alignment beats script.

The Momentum Protocol

Start with coalition before strategy. Who you have on your side determines what's possible.

Select pilot projects that matter enough to engage talent but aren't so critical that failure would be catastrophic. Set aggressive but achievable timelines and ensure urgency without panic.

Measure momentum through leading indicators—volunteer participation; organic advocacy. When people opt in rather than comply, transformation has taken hold.

Making It Work: Identify one transformation effort that's losing steam. Apply the four steps:

1. Reconnect to genuine purpose beyond metrics.
2. Architect a ninety-day win proving progress is possible.
3. Build a coalition extending beyond the usual suspects.
4. Establish narrative discipline that puts an end to mixed messages.

Track whether energy increases or continues declining. Create conditions where transformation feels inevitable, not impossible.

Framework 3: The Sticky Change Protocol (Governance, routines and guardrails that stick)

Most transformations achieve initial success, but then the organisation gradually reverts to old patterns. Leaders focus on launching change rather than embedding it in the fabric of their team.

This method builds mechanisms that make transformation self-sustaining rather than leader-dependent. Stop babysitting change. Start engineering permanence.

Step 1: Embed Change in Daily Operations

The critical mistake: treating transformation as a parallel initiative rather than integrated reality. When transformation requires extra effort beyond regular work, it dies the moment attention shifts. Make transformation stick through operational integration:

- Redesign workflows so the new way becomes the only way
- Update systems so old processes no longer function
- Restructure metrics so performance requires transformation
- Revise roles so reverting means failing core responsibilities

When the transformed approach becomes the path of least resistance, the question changes from 'Will we maintain this?' to 'Why would we go backward?'.

Step 2: Build Distributed Capability

Transformations collapse when knowledge is concentrated in a few experts who become bottlenecks or departure risks. Sustainable change requires making expertise abundant, not scarce.

Create widespread capability:

- Teach others to teach, not just perform
- Document why, not just how
- Rotate knowledge across teams through programmes
- Build communities of practice that evolve methods collectively

The test: Can teams adapt and improve independently? When innovation comes from the edges rather than the centre, transformation has truly taken root.

Step 3: Establish Cultural Reinforcement

Culture determines whether transformation lasts or fades. And in creating culture, daily behaviours matter more than declared strategies.

Build cultural sustainability through:

- Recognition systems celebrating transformation behaviours
- Promotion criteria requiring transformation leadership
- Story systems making transformation part of identity
- Peer accountability making regression socially costly

When career advancement requires transformation leadership rather than traditional excellence, cultural reinforcement becomes self-executing.

Step 4: Create Measurement That Matters

Organisations inevitably move towards what they measure. Yet most transformation metrics track activities rather than outcomes.

Design measurement through three levels:

- *Leading indicators*: These predict success before it arrives.
- *Outcome metrics*: These confirm value delivery.
- *Sustainability markers*: These indicate lasting change.

Avoid measuring everything that moves. Choose fewer metrics that actually indicate transformation health rather than comprehensive dashboards no one uses.

The Sustainability Protocol

Install sustainability mechanisms during transformation, not after. Habits form early. Make the transformed state feel normal rather than special. Integrate the change into routine operations rather than celebrating it as being exceptional.

To test sustainability, remove active support. Does transformation continue or degrade? Real sustainability means the organisation pulls transformation forward rather than leadership pushing it.

Making It Work: Select one successful pilot that needs to scale. Apply the sustainability system: redesign operations, making the new approach standard. Identify five people who can teach others independently. Create recognition that celebrates adoption of the new systems. Establish three metrics indicating genuine sustainability.

Gradually reduce oversight. Monitor whether transformation strengthens or weakens. The goal is that reverting should require more effort than continuing.

The three frameworks provide structure, but transformation efforts hit predictable obstacles. Understanding these pitfalls will help you navigate around them rather than learning through expensive failure.

Common Transformation Pitfalls (and Why Smart Leaders Fall into Them)

Smart, well-meaning leaders fall into predictable traps, especially when implementation speed and complexity are at loggerheads. Based on my experience, here are five pitfalls that show up repeatedly:

1. Tech-First Thinking

Shiny new tools are tempting. They're tangible and come with impressive dashboards. But transformation isn't about technology, it's about what people do with it. Without behavioural change, even the best tools fall flat. I've watched organisations spend millions on platforms that became expensive dust collectors.

Excel spreadsheets with engaged users beat sophisticated systems people work around.

2. Change Overload

Organisations can only absorb so much disruption before they shut down. Push too hard and you get resistance, fatigue and malicious compliance. Leaders excited about the future forget that their teams are buried in yesterday's deadlines while delivering today's results.

Human capacity for change is finite. Exceed it, and even good transformations fail.

3. Communication Fatigue

Too little communication breeds anxiety. Too much creates noise people tune out. Teams don't need daily transformation newsletters or motivational emails. They need timely, relevant clarity about what's actually changing for them.

Communicate with purpose, not frequency. Answer the questions people have, not the ones you wish they would ask.

4. Ignoring the Human Side

Most transformation decks are full of workflows and milestones. Few account for fear, loss and identity shifts. The engineer who built the legacy system sees decommissioning as career erasure. The team that perfected the old process experiences improvement as criticism. These are common human responses.

Until leaders acknowledge emotional reality, resistance keeps surfacing in unexpected ways.

5. Short-Term Pressure Override

Transformation takes time. But when quarterly targets dip or leaders rotate out, initiatives get paused or quietly abandoned. This sends an unmistakable message: transformation was optional all along. Once momentum is lost, rebuilding trust takes exponentially longer than maintaining it would have.

Signalling Leadership Readiness

If you're aiming for leadership roles, your ability to lead transformation becomes the primary differentiator. Senior leaders look for specific evidence that you can handle enterprise-scale change. Your transformation portfolio tells a story about readiness. Decision-makers look for patterns across multiple transformations, not single successes.

They evaluate four patterns:

- *Complexity progression*: How you progress from departmental to cross-functional to enterprise-wide impact
- *Value creation*: How much measurable business value you add beyond operational metrics
- *Capability legacy*: To what extent you have strengthened the organisation's transformation muscle

- *Stakeholder trust*: Whether people volunteer to join rather than being assigned to your initiatives

The Five Signals That Matter

1. *Delivery consistency.* You complete transformations on time and within scope without leaving organisational carnage. This isn't about perfect execution but predictable delivery that builds confidence.
2. *Authentic followership.* People join because they believe in the vision, not the mandate. The difference between compliance and commitment shows when you're not in the room.
3. *Organisational strengthening.* Your transformations leave enhanced capability, not just changed processes. Teams tackle the next change better because of what they learnt from yours.
4. *Change leadership trust.* When the board faces critical transformation, your name comes up naturally. You're trusted with changes that can't fail, not just ones that might succeed.
5. *Strategic pattern recognition.* You see opportunities others miss and risks others underestimate. Your read on what works in your specific context proves to be consistently accurate.

The real value of these frameworks isn't simplifying complexity but harnessing it systematically. Transformation capability separates managers who maintain operations from leaders who reshape enterprises. Your transformation track record becomes the clearest signal of leadership readiness.

Master transformation, and the promotions find you.

23

View from the Top with Vivek Gambhir

To understand what transformation leadership looks like at the top, I asked Vivek Gambhir, partner at Lightspeed Ventures and former CEO of Godrej Consumer Products and boAt Lifestyle.[1] *Vivek has led business model transformations across large consumer goods and the entrepreneurial ecosystem. I had the privilege of co-authoring my first book,* HeadStart, *with Vivek, and wanted his perspective on what he looks for when identifying managers ready to lead enterprise-scale change. Here's what he had to say.*

Real transformation isn't about changing structures or organisational charts. It's about changing energy, how people think, feel and show up every day. It begins quietly in the questions managers ask, the stories they tell and the behaviours they tolerate. The best leaders don't just design change. They make people believe that something better is possible and that they have a role in building it.

What Signals Transformation Readiness

When I assess a manager's readiness to lead transformation, I look for leaders who have started asking bigger questions. Not

---

1 See 'Vivek Gambhir,' LinkedIn, https://in.linkedin.com/in/vivek-gambhir-b955a836.

just 'How do we get it done?' but 'Why are we doing this?'. They connect dots across silos and care about outcomes beyond their function. They don't just manage work. They help others make sense of it.

I also notice how they respond when things go off-script. Do they get defensive or stay curious? Do they blame, or do they learn? The ones who can stay grounded amid ambiguity and still bring others along are the ones ready to move from delivering results to shaping culture.

The First 90–120 Days

The best leaders begin with humility. They take time to understand the pulse, what excites people, what worries them, what stories are circulating. They build trust before building plans. In the early days, they focus on a few visible wins that restore belief that progress is possible. But they also protect the team's energy by being honest about trade-offs, by celebrating small steps and by creating space to breathe.

In fast-moving situations, they balance clarity with compassion. They don't have all the answers. And they admit it. That honesty itself builds credibility and momentum.

What Makes Transformation Stick

Change endures when it starts feeling personal. When people see the new behaviours rewarded, the new language mirrored in meetings and the new values reflected in decisions, it begins to stick. Metrics matter. But stories matter more. The rituals, small signals and leader behaviours make transformation real.

I've learnt that rhythm beats intensity. What keeps change alive isn't one big launch or offsite. It's the steady drumbeat that follows, the small conversations, the check-ins, the willingness to listen and course-correct. Real change seeps into habits before it shows up in results.

And you know it's worked when people stop talking about the transformation altogether. It's just the way things are done now. No fanfare, no labels—just quiet consistency.

The Operator Challenge

The most common pitfall I see is that strong operators are wired to deliver, plan, control and execute. But transformation can't be controlled. It has to be guided.

Many strong performers struggle because what made them successful earlier—control, precision, speed—starts working against them. They try to run transformation like a well-oiled project, expecting predictability where there is none. I tell them to think less like project managers and more like orchestra conductors. Their job isn't to play every instrument. It's to create harmony. That means stepping back, listening more and trusting others to take the lead on different notes.

The real test of leadership isn't how much you drive, but how much you can let go without losing the rhythm. When that shift happens, people stop waiting for direction and start owning the change. That's when momentum becomes real.

24

Do-It Notes: Your Transformation Road Map

Now it's time to convert transformation insights into deliberate practice. The core question isn't 'How do I manage change better?', it's 'How do I architect transformation that builds momentum rather than resistance, creates capability rather than dependency and delivers results that outlast my involvement?'.

Mindsets Over Structures

'Transformation is not about changing structures. It is about changing mindsets.'

—*Nandan Nilekani*

Do-It Notes

This Month: Diagnose Your Readiness

1. *Document your transformation baseline.* Write a brief reflection on your last change leadership experience. What would your team say about how you led? What would you do differently? This becomes your starting point.

Do-It Notes: Your Transformation Road Map

2. *Run a change capacity audit.* What major changes occurred in the last twelve months? Where is energy high versus depleted? What would break if you added another significant change? Document the reality, not the wish.
3. *Map your stakeholder readiness.* Identify ten critical stakeholders. Plot their influence level. Assess their change enthusiasm. Document what they gain or lose. Know your allies and obstacles.
4. *Evaluate implementation complexity.* Score your transformation across five dimensions: technical integration, functional coordination, process interdependencies, behavioural change magnitude, external timeline pressures. Underestimating complexity kills transformations.

This Quarter: Build Transformation Architecture

1. *Launch your pilot initiative.* Choose a painful but solvable problem everyone recognises. Recruit ten willing participants. Set ninety-day metrics that matter to the business. Document lessons weekly, not just at the end.
2. *Create your coalition structure.* Build support across four layers:
   - Core team: Daily execution ownership
   - Champions: Barrier removal and resource access
   - Early adopters: Proof it works
   - Amplifiers: Story spreading

   The design outlasts the people.
3. *Design momentum mechanisms.* Plan reinforcement that compounds:
   - Thirty days: Quick win proving possibility
   - Sixty days: Expansion showing scalability
   - Ninety days: Integration demonstrating sustainability

   Make progress visible to everyone.

4. *Establish narrative discipline.* Have one core message every leader reinforces. Share weekly progress featuring real stories, not just metrics. Create monthly forums for genuine dialogue. Alignment beats volume.

This Year: Scale Transformation Excellence

1. *Lead an enterprise transformation.* Demonstrate capability at scale through one major initiative: digital transformation across business units; business model evolution across markets; operational excellence with P&L impact. Prove you can handle enterprise complexity.
2. *Build organisational capability.* Create transformation muscle that outlasts you. Run quarterly workshops teaching your methods. Create peer learning communities. Mentor two managers through their first transformations. Your legacy is the leaders you develop.
3. *Create sustainability systems.* Design change that sticks without you. Embed new approaches into workflows. Build distributed expertise. Establish cultural reinforcement through recognition. Make the new way easier than the old way.
4. *Track your transformation portfolio.* Document impact systematically. Track the number of successful transformations led, the scope and scale achieved, your speed compared to benchmarks, the leaders you have developed. This becomes your promotion ammunition.

The Non-Negotiables

Three practices that build transformation excellence:

- *Weekly*: The readiness pulse (twenty minutes). Review capacity, stakeholder positions, complexity. Course-correct before problems become crises.
- *Monthly*: The momentum check (one hour). Assess energy, resistance, narrative consistency. Intervene when momentum stalls.
- *Quarterly*: The sustainability audit (two hours). Evaluate what's self-sustaining versus requiring push. Redesign what depends on heroic effort.

You'll know it's working when:

- Transformations deliver without your constant oversight
- People volunteer for your initiatives
- Other leaders adopt your methods
- Your organisation handles subsequent changes better
- You're trusted with critical transformations

The ultimate sign? You're asked to lead the transformation that can't fail.

Your Turn Now

The VALUES Framework has prepared you for the leap. You've seen the stories. You have the tools. You've worked through the 'how'.

Now it's about choosing the 'when'. The question isn't whether you're ready. It's how you'll use your leadership to build something that lasts.

Conclusion

Thank you for reading this.

As I reflect on writing this book, Winston Churchill's words about authorship feel particularly apt: 'Writing a book is an adventure. To begin with it is a toy and an amusement. Then it becomes a mistress, then it becomes a master, then it becomes a tyrant. The last phase is that just as you are about to be reconciled to your servitude, you kill the monster and fling him to the public.'

This book felt like that. The only way through was to show up and keep going.

How the VALUES Framework Works Together

The six capabilities build on each other. Start with whatever's hitting you hardest right now, then expand.

- **Volatility**: Move fast with incomplete information.
- **Anchored in Values**: Your compass when speed creates pressure.
- **Leveraging Global–Local Dynamics**: Translate between competing demands.
- **Unique Reputation**: Makes you visible and in demand.
- **Exceptional Teams**: Multiply your impact beyond yourself.

- **Sustainable Transformation**: Reshape systems, not just work within them.

Returning to Where We Started

In the introduction, I asked you three questions. Let me help you answer them through the lens of what you've learnt.

1. Which leaders in your organisation do you admire, and why?

You likely admire them because they've mastered several VALUES capabilities. They move through volatility without panicking. They stick to principles while delivering results. Their reputation arrives before they do. Now you have the frameworks.

2. What would you need to change about yourself to compete for the next level?

The answer usually hides in the capability that felt most uncomfortable as you read. That discomfort tells you where you need to grow.

3. If you were promoted tomorrow, what would you stop doing?

This reveals what doesn't scale. Stop being the hero who solves every problem. Stop perfecting work others should own. Stop waiting for permission to act.

Your Next Thirty Days

Here's your next move:

- *Within Forty-eight hours*: Take one concrete action from the Do-It Notes. Just one. Send that email. Map that tension. Run that audit. Start that pilot. Don't wait for the perfect moment.

- *Within two weeks*: Identify someone one step ahead of you. Not a CEO, not an inspiration from afar, but someone who recently made the leap you're contemplating. Buy them coffee. Ask specific questions. Learn from recent experience.
- *Within thirty days*: Become visible for something that matters. Present your own work. Own your narrative. Step into that stretch assignment. Raise your hand for the transformation everyone else is avoiding.

Make yourself uncomfortable.

If I could leave you with one last piece of advice: don't do this alone. When you figure out something that works, share it with someone coming up behind you. Teaching cements the lesson.

You're closer to that leadership role than you think. The frameworks are here. The path is mapped. Take the next step.

If this book helped, I'd like to hear from you. Write to me at sunder.ramachandran@gmail.com, or connect on linkedin.com/in/sundertrg.

Acknowledgements

I have been lucky to work with leaders who took a chance on me before I was ready. They taught me that titles come and go, but how you think and lead stays with you:

- Vivek Gambhir, Partner, Lightspeed Ventures
- Mahima Datla, Managing Director, Biological E. Limited
- Bhushan Akshikar, Managing Director, GSK Pharmaceuticals Ltd
- Sridhar Venkatesh, President, GSK Canada
- Annaswamy Vaidheesh, former Managing Director, GSK Pharmaceuticals and J&J
- Somer Tayyareci, senior Global Marketing Director, GSK
- Anil Iyer, former Chief Commercial Officer, GSK Pharmaceuticals Ltd.
- Savita Bradoo Joshi, Chief Operating Officer, Tek Experts
- M.V. Ramana, CEO, India and Emerging Markets, Dr. Reddy's Laboratories
- Ronald Sequeira, former Executive Director, HR, GSK Pharmaceuticals Ltd
- Hariram Krishnan, former Managing Director, Galderma Pharma India
- Rajeev Bartaria, former EVP, GSK Pharmaceuticals Ltd.

Acknowledgements

To my editor, Aurodeep Mukherjee, and my publishing partners at Westland Books: thank you for making this book happen.

To Vasundhara Sawhney, former editor at *Harvard Business Review*: thank you for the detailed review that made this book sharper and more useful.

To the mid-career professionals I've coached: this book exists because of your questions, your struggles with feeling stuck and your ambition to lead at the enterprise level. Kavita, Arjun and Priya are composites from those conversations.

To my wife, Deeksha: thank you for your patience, unconditional love and support.

To my daughter, Veda: I hope you grow up in a world where your ambitions have no ceiling, and may you never feel stuck for long.

And to you, the reader: thank you for picking this up. I hope you come back to it when you're stuck.